lessons
from
David

lessons from
David

Adanna Phillip

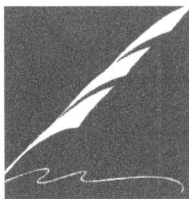

CONCLUSIO
HOUSE PUBLISHING

"Lessons from David: A Study of the Life of King David"

REL012020 **RELIGION**/Christian Life/Devotional
REL012120 **RELIGION**/Christian Life/Spiritual Growth

Printed in Canada
First Printing, 2017

ISBN 978-1-988847-03-0

Published by:
Conclusio House Publishing
Brampton, Ontario
Canada
www.conclusiohouse.com

I dedicate this book to my family, and to my church, Faith United Ministries. Thank you for the solid foundation, unconditional love, and incessant prayers.

Acknowledgements

I give honour to the Holy Spirit, my teacher. Thank you for the vision, divine leading, and inspiration. The depth of your revelation is simply awesome. I love that you use the foolish things of the earth to confound the wise (1 Corinthians 1:27). That qualified me. There is no greater honour, and nothing more humbling, than being used for the glory of God.

I bless God for my family. Thank you to my huge extended family of amazing aunts, uncles, cousins, nieces, and nephews. Our family has inspired me on my spiritual journey. What the enemy meant for evil, God has turned around for good. Thank you for your unfailing support.

To my deceased grandmother, Ruth Greenaway, my mother, Glyris Edwards, my aunt Glenda Wyllis, my sisters, Shennel Edwards and Latoya Foster, and my brothers, Rudy Phillip and Shannim Phillip, thank you for always believing in me, always supporting my dreams, and for the pride I always see in your eyes and hear in your voices. Words cannot express how grateful I am to have you in my life.

My church is such an amazing support. Thank you to my pastor, my mentor, and my spiritual father, Bishop Dr. Kenneth G. Fuller. Your encouragement, wisdom, and genuine care for those you pastor are priceless. Your standards of excellence and your high expectations of yourself and others, especially when it comes to the things of God, inspire me to excel. To my church mothers, my prayer warriors, and the wonderful youth at Faith United Ministries, I can't imagine this journey without you. Thank you for your encouragement, your love, and your constant prayer covering. I love and appreciate you.

Thank you to everyone who had some part to play in this work and in my life. May the Lord bless you beyond every expectation.

Table of Contents

Introduction

"After removing Saul, he made David their king. God testified concerning him: 'I have found David son of Jesse, a man after my own heart; he will do everything I want him to do'" (Acts 13:22 NIV).

What an honour for God Himself to call you a man after His own heart. This sort of privileged place in the heart and thoughts of God is one that is surely desired by every saint who reads of it. What gave David, a little shepherd boy, living in obscurity, not notable in any way—not even to his own family—such a place in the heart of God? What can we learn from the life of David through Scripture that will teach us what attributes, qualities, and behaviours made God hold David in such high regard? It turns out that there is a lot to learn from the Books of Samuel that can propel believers into the will of God. In Acts 13:22, God says of David, *"He will do everything I want him to do."*

So what did David do? How did he live? I love David. The truth is I have a particular soft spot for people in the Bible, like David and Peter, who are zealous and passionate about the things of God, who really love God, but who still end up failing Him sometimes. These sorts of men remind me so much of myself, and the immense grace that God bestowed upon them secures my faith in the depth of God's grace.

One of the most notable things about David and his relationship with God is how open and candid He was. David said, and truly believed, that God would not despise a broken and contrite heart (Psalm 51:17). David lived his life being brutally open and honest with God. He never pretended to be more than he was, more righteous than he was, or even more spiritual and encouraged than he was. David realized something that we all ought to realize: you cannot pretend with God. I implore you, as you read through this book, to peel through the layers, facades, pretences of your own life, and be open and honest with God. As David often did in the compilation of Psalms, state honestly how you feel, then make your statement of faith and express confidence in the Word and power of God to take you from where you are to where you ought to be.

That David, the man whom God gave the highest commendation in Scripture, after his Son and Peter, the man of whom Christ said, *"Upon this rock I will build my church,"* was not perfect, and was in fact very human, gives me hope that I'm not counted out. So I seek to learn from David—his strengths, his weaknesses, his failures, his victories, his flaws, and his virtues. I choose to allow him to mentor me. The following compilation, from 1 and 2 Samuel, is by no means an exhaustive list of the lessons to be learned from the life of David. The following key lessons are merely the ones that are most salient to me, for now.

lessons
from
David

Small Beginnings

1 Samuel 16

The Lᴏʀᴅ said to Samuel, "How long will you mourn for Saul, since I have rejected him as king over Israel? Fill your horn with oil and be on your way; I am sending you to Jesse of Bethlehem. I have chosen one of his sons to be king." But Samuel said, "How can I go? If Saul hears about it, he will kill me."

The Lᴏʀᴅ said, "Take a heifer with you and say, 'I have come to sacrifice to the Lᴏʀᴅ.' Invite Jesse to the sacrifice, and I will show you what to do. You are to anoint for me the one I indicate." Samuel did what the Lᴏʀᴅ said. When he arrived at Bethlehem, the elders of the town trembled when they met him. They asked, "Do you come in peace?"

Samuel replied, "Yes, in peace; I have come to sacrifice to the Lᴏʀᴅ. Consecrate yourselves and come to the sacrifice with me." Then he consecrated Jesse and his sons and invited them to the sacrifice. When they arrived, Samuel saw Eliab and thought, "Surely the Lᴏʀᴅ's anointed stands here before the Lᴏʀᴅ."

But the Lᴏʀᴅ said to Samuel, "Do not consider his appearance or his height, for I have rejected him. The Lᴏʀᴅ does not look at the things people look at. People look at the outward appearance, but the LORD looks at the heart." Then Jesse called Abinadab and had him pass in front of Samuel. But Samuel said, "The LORD has not chosen this one either." Jesse then had Shammah pass by, but Samuel said, "Nor has the LORD chosen this one." Jesse had seven of his sons pass before Samuel, but Samuel said to him, "The LORD has not chosen these." ¹¹ So he asked Jesse, "Are these all the sons you have?"

"There is still the youngest," Jesse answered. "He is tending the sheep." Samuel said, "Send for him; we will not sit down until he arrives." So he sent for him and had him brought in. He was glowing with health and had a fine appearance and handsome features. Then the LORD said, "Rise and anoint him; this is the one."

So Samuel took the horn of oil and anointed him in the presence of his brothers, and from that day on the Spirit of the LORD came powerfully upon David. Samuel then went to Ramah. Now the Spirit of the LORD had departed from Saul, and an evil spirit from the LORD tormented him.

Saul's attendants said to him, "See, an evil spirit from God is tormenting you. Let our lord command his servants here to search for someone who can play the lyre. He will play when the evil spirit from God comes on you, and you will feel better." So Saul said to his attendants, "Find someone who plays well and bring him to me." One of the servants answered, "I have seen a son of Jesse of Bethlehem who knows how to play the lyre. He is a brave man and a warrior. He speaks well and is a fine-looking man. And the LORD is with him."

Then Saul sent messengers to Jesse and said, "Send me your son David, who is with the sheep." So Jesse took a donkey loaded with bread, a skin of wine and a young goat and sent them with his son David to Saul.

David came to Saul and entered his service. Saul liked him

very much, and David became one of his armor-bearers. Then Saul sent word to Jesse, saying, "Allow David to remain in my service, for I am pleased with him." Whenever the spirit from God came on Saul, David would take up his lyre and play. Then relief would come to Saul; he would feel better, and the evil spirit would leave him.

(1 Samuel 16 NIV)

David's life is an excellent example of a person's beginning not dictating the course of his life. Our mentor starts out in the field, clearly the least of his father's household. David's beginning was so unimpressive that he never crossed his father's mind as a potential candidate for king among his sons. Even more profound, his father did not even consider it necessary for him to see one of his brothers anointed as king. He was left outside doing the menial grunge work, but that same, unimpressive David was God's chosen and would be the greatest king of Israel.

The Bible tells us that we are not to despise small beginnings. While David's beginning seemed small and menial, it is not until we get further into his story that God reveals how He was using that beginning to prune and process David to prepare him for kingship. From leading his father's sheep to leading God's chosen people; from slaying bears and lions to slaying giants and earning a formidable reputation as a mighty, valiant man and a man of war (1 Samuel 16:1).

You may be in a place where you are working hard, seeking God with your whole heart, but it seems as though no one notices. Take heart, this is not the end of your story; it is only the beginning. God is pruning you and preparing you for what lies ahead. *"For I know the thoughts I think towards you, says the Lord, thoughts of peace and not of evil, to give you a future and a hope"* (Jeremiah 29:11). Be encouraged, because *"Eyes have not seen and ears have not heard, nor has it entered into the heart of man the things that God has in store for them that fear Him"* (1 Corinthians 2:9). Do not despise your small beginning, for it does not dictate your future.

Prayer: Lord, give me grace to be patient and pliable as you work out your divine will in my life. Prune and process me at will, in whatever way and whatever place you choose. Prepare and position me to serve you fully in your divine will and calling for my life. Amen.

Behaving Wisely

1 Samuel 18:5–16

And David went out whithersoever Saul sent him, and behaved himself wisely: and Saul set him over the men of war, and he was accepted in the sight of all the people, and also in the sight of Saul's servants. And it came to pass as they came, when David was returned from the slaughter of the Philistine, that the women came out of all cities of Israel, singing and dancing, to meet king Saul, with tabrets, with joy, and with instruments of musick.

And the women answered one another as they played, and said, Saul hath slain his thousands, and David his ten thousands. And Saul was very wroth, and the saying displeased him; and he said, They have ascribed unto David ten thousands, and to me they have ascribed but thousands: and what can he have more but the kingdom?

And Saul eyed David from that day and forward. And it came to pass on the morrow, that the evil spirit from God came upon Saul, and he prophesied in the midst of the house: and David played with his hand, as at other times: and there was a javelin in Saul's hand.

And Saul cast the javelin; for he said, I will smite David even to the wall with it. And David avoided out of his presence twice. And Saul was afraid of David, because the LORD was with him, and was departed from Saul. Therefore Saul removed him from him, and made him his captain over a thousand; and he went out and came in before the people.

And David behaved himself wisely in all his ways; and the LORD was with him. Wherefore when Saul saw that he behaved himself very wisely, he was afraid of him. But all Israel and Judah loved David, because he went out and came in before them.

(1 Samuel 18:5-16)

───◆◇◇◆───

The Bible says that Saul became jealous of David, even to the point of attempted murder. And David? He "behaved himself wisely" (1 Samuel 18:5). We know that it is extremely difficult to act with wisdom and to be prudent in our dealings when things are not going well and we feel as though we are being wronged or treated unfairly. For me, "behaving wisely," in its literal sense, is extremely challenging to do when things are not working my way or when I'm not happy. But the ability to behave wisely in cruel conditions is an awesome measure of spiritual maturity. Many times, we go through a trial without recognizing it as a test—a test of spiritual maturity, a test to reveal our true selves. There is an old saying that goes "A woman is like a tea bag, you never know how strong she is until you put her in hot water." I dare to say that that's applicable for us as Christians. You never know how strong or weak you are until you are tested with trials. How you deal with trials is also a clear indication and manifestation of the fruit of the indwelling Holy Spirit, according to Galatians 5:22–23. Being long-suffering and exercising self-control, despite the situation, is incredibly mature.

Too often, our behaviour is dictated by our circumstances. Too often, we are tossed and turned and controlled by what is going on around us. But the Bible says that a person without self-control is like a city broken down and without walls (Proverbs 25:28 NLT). A person without self-control, like a city without walls, is in a very vulnerable position, because the enemy can go in and out at will. In ancient days, the walls around the city were for protection and fortification, to keep the enemy out. They were a sign of strength. Therefore, to be without walls—self-control—is extremely dangerous. Our enemy knows our weaknesses, and if we have no control over ourselves, then he will control us at will by bringing certain situations into our lives to make us act outside of the will of God. Imagine being controlled by the enemy.

Some translations of the Bible say that David prospered in all that He did. Incredibly, God chose to elevate David, even in such tense and tumultuous situations. Talk about spreading a table before us in the presence of our enemies. I do not know that David would have prospered or would have been blessed in all he did had he not behaved himself wisely. Be assured that there is great reward for those who choose to behave Christ-like, regardless of their circumstances.

Prayer: Lord, give me grace to behave myself wisely, despite my circumstances. Amen.

Christ-Positioned Allies

1 Samuel 19

And Saul spake to Jonathan his son, and to all his servants, that they should kill David. But Jonathan Saul's son delighted much in David: and Jonathan told David, saying, Saul my father seeketh to kill thee: now therefore, I pray thee, take heed to thyself until the morning, and abide in a secret place, and hide thyself: And I will go out and stand beside my father in the field where thou art, and I will commune with my father of thee; and what I see, that I will tell thee. And Jonathan spake good of David unto Saul his father, and said unto him, Let not the king sin against his servant, against David; because he hath not sinned against thee, and because his works have been to thee-ward very good: For he did put his life in his hand, and slew the Philistine, and the LORD wrought a great salvation for all Israel: thou sawest it, and didst rejoice: wherefore then wilt thou sin against innocent blood, to slay David without a cause? And Saul hearkened unto the voice of Jonathan: and Saul sware, As the LORD liveth, he shall not be slain. And Jonathan called David, and Jonathan shewed him all those things. And Jonathan brought David to Saul, and he was in his presence, as in times past. And there was war again: and David went out, and fought with the Philistines, and slew them with a great slaughter; and they fled from him. And the evil spirit from the LORD was upon Saul, as he sat in his house with his javelin in his hand: and David played with his hand. And Saul sought to smite David even to the wall with the javelin: but he slipped away out of Saul's presence, and he smote the javelin into the wall: and David fled, and escaped that night. Saul also sent messengers unto David's house, to watch him, and to slay him in the morning: and Michal David's wife told him, saying, If thou save not thy life to night, to morrow thou shalt be slain.

So Michal let David down through a window: and he went, and fled, and escaped. And Michal took an image, and laid it in the bed, and put a pillow of goats' hair for his bolster, and covered it with a cloth.

And when Saul sent messengers to take David, she said, He is sick. And Saul sent the messengers again to see David, saying, Bring him up to me in the bed, that I may slay him. And when the messengers were come in, behold, there was an image in the bed, with a pillow of goats' hair for his bolster. And Saul said unto Michal, Why hast thou deceived me so, and sent away mine enemy, that he is escaped? And Michal answered Saul, He said unto me, Let me go; why should I kill thee?

So David fled, and escaped, and came to Samuel to Ramah, and told him all that Saul had done to him. And he and Samuel went and dwelt in Naioth. And it was told Saul, saying, Behold, David is at Naioth in Ramah. And Saul sent messengers to take David: and when they saw the company of the prophets prophesying, and Samuel standing as appointed over them, the Spirit of God was upon the messengers of Saul, and they also prophesied. And when it was told Saul, he sent other messengers, and they prophesied likewise. And Saul sent messengers again the third time, and they prophesied also.

Then went he also to Ramah, and came to a great well

that is in Sechu: and he asked and said, Where are Samuel and David? And one said, Behold, they be at Naioth in Ramah. And he went thither to Naioth in Ramah: and the Spirit of God was upon him also, and he went on, and prophesied, until he came to Naioth in Ramah. And he stripped off his clothes also, and prophesied before Samuel in like manner, and lay down naked all that day and all that night. Wherefore they say, Is Saul also among the prophets?

(1 Samuel 19)

❖

It is amazing that David's greatest allies were Saul's own flesh and blood. God ordained for both Michal and Jonathan to love their father's biggest enemy, and gave him favour with them, so as to preserve David's life. He took loyalty that should have been Saul's away from him and gave it to David. Saul made Michal marry David in order to ensnare him and lead him to his demise, but she saved his life from her father instead. Like God often does, what David's enemy meant for evil, God turned completely around for his good.

God puts allies in unlikely places. We ought not to be too caught up with knowing people on the surface; instead, we should desire to know their hearts. David could have been turned off merely by the fact that Jonathan and Michal were Saul's children. He could have avoided them, withdrawn his friendship and affection, and even refused to trust them, but he did not, and they saved his life multiple times against the wishes of their own father. For many of us, this is definitely a lesson in terms of dealing with people whom we view as our enemies. We have a tendency to generalize the enemy. We may have been hurt or mistreated by a certain person or group, and, in self-preservation mode, we put our guards up with everyone associated with, or who reminds us of, that person or group.

The honest truth is that many of us have deep-rooted trust issues. However, we need to trust God to lead us to the right people and to give us favour in unlikely places. We need to stop trying to preserve ourselves, and ask God for His wisdom. I remember debating with God when I sensed Him doing some work around my hurts and my mistrust of certain people. I said to Him, "Lord, it won't work, because I don't trust them." Immediately, the Spirit of God said to me, "I'm not asking you to trust them. I'm asking you to trust Me." Yes, I did have a comeback—albeit a weak one—"Lord, I do trust you, but you give everyone freewill, so if they choose to hurt me again, they can." But in true omniscience, He had deposited His truth in my spirit, and He was done. God is not asking you to put your trust in mortals; He is asking you to trust Him. Stop trying to protect yourself; you risk missing out on some God-ordained allies and relationships that are tied to your destiny. Take down your self-constructed walls, and allow Him to build a fence around you and protect you.

Prayer: Lord, help me to be wise and vigilant. Help me to not make judgements based on outward appearances or generalizations. Heal my wounded heart and help me to trust you and to be led by you, in Jesus' name. Amen.

Trusting God

1 Samuel 21

Then came David to Nob to Ahimelech the priest: and Ahimelech was afraid at the meeting of David, and said unto him, Why art thou alone, and no man with thee? And David said unto Ahimelech the priest, The king hath commanded me a business, and hath said unto me, Let no man know any thing of the business whereabout I send thee, and what I have commanded thee: and I have appointed my servants to such and such a place. Now therefore what is under thine hand? give me five loaves of bread in mine hand, or what there is present. And the priest answered David, and said, There is no common bread under mine hand, but there is hallowed bread; if the young men have kept themselves at least from women. And David answered the priest, and said unto him, Of a truth women have been kept from us about these three days, since I came out, and the vessels of the young men are holy, and the bread is in a manner common, yea, though it were sanctified this day in the vessel.

So the priest gave him hallowed bread: for there was no bread there but the shewbread, that was taken from before the LORD, *to put hot bread in the day when it was taken away. Now a certain man of the servants of Saul was there that day, detained before the* LORD; *and his name was Doeg, an Edomite, the chiefest of the herdmen that belonged to Saul. And David said unto Ahimelech,*

And is there not here under thine hand spear or sword? for I have neither brought my sword nor my weapons with me, because the king's business required haste. And the priest said, The sword of Goliath the Philistine, whom thou slewest in the valley of Elah, behold, it is here wrapped in a cloth behind the ephod: if thou wilt take that, take it: for there is no other save that here. And David said, There is none like that; give it me. And David arose and fled that day for fear of Saul, and went to Achish the king of Gath. And the servants of Achish said unto him, Is not this David the king of the land? did they not sing one to another of him in dances, saying, Saul hath slain his thousands, and David his ten thousands? And David laid up these words in his heart, and was sore afraid of Achish the king of Gath. And he changed his behaviour before them, and feigned himself mad in their hands, and scrabbled on the doors of the gate, and let his spittle fall down upon his beard. Then said Achish unto his servants, Lo, ye see the man is mad: wherefore then have ye brought him to me? Have I need of mad men, that ye have brought this fellow to play the mad man in my presence? shall this fellow come into my house?

(1 Samuel 21)

David lied multiple times to save his life. This might have be an indication that he was not depending on the Lord to see Him through, but rather on his own strength. Sometimes we get into telling "white lies" or "lies for the greater good," but this is not the way of God. If God wants to get you out of a situation or to make a way for you, He can and will do so, without your intervention. He never ordains sinning against Him.

All of us, at some point in life, will face, or have faced, threatening circumstances in which we are scared for our safety and security. When we are, we have a choice to make. David, here, was understandably scared for his life, and he made a choice to preserve his life by his own strength and cunning. There is a stark contrast between David and Shadrach, Meshach, and Abednego (Daniel 3). They refused to compromise or use their own strategies to deter the threat of a sordid death. Even when the furnace was turned up seven times hotter, they refused to compromise or sin against their God. The three Hebrew boys fully trusted that if it was God's will to save their lives, they would be saved, and as such, their ingenuity was not necessary for their deliverance. David can also be contrasted to Daniel (Daniel 6), who refused to compromise and sin against his God by not praying. Even when he knew the threat of the lion's den was very real, he still prayed and did not compromise his beliefs.

In both the aforementioned cases, God's deliverance of those who relied on Him, and not on deception or lies, to preserve their lives, was amazing, and all the glory went to God. Because His awesome power to save was brilliantly displayed, the testimonies of those delivered still inspire and encourage believers thousands of years later. When we try to help God, we are distracting the world from seeing His glory, and robbing ourselves of a testimony.

(Also read Psalms 34 and 56, their historical background is 1 Samuel 21)

Prayer: Father in Heaven, help me to put my trust in you and not to lean on my own understanding. Let not self-preservation trump my pursuit of righteousness and my desire to please you. God, I trust that if it is your will to deliver me, you are omnipotent and, as such, well able to help me. I pray that whatever role I need to play will be revealed to me by your Holy Spirit, in Jesus' name. Amen.

The Ways of God (1):
A Message to Our Insecurities

1 Samuel 22:1–4; 23:1–5

David therefore departed thence, and escaped to the cave Adullam: and when his brethren and all his father's house heard it, they went down thither to him.

And every one that was in distress, and every one that was in debt, and every one that was discontented, gathered themselves unto him; and he became a captain over them: and there were with him about four hundred men.

And David went thence to Mizpeh of Moab: and he said unto the king of Moab, Let my father and my mother, I pray thee, come forth, and be with you, till I know what God will do for me.

And he brought them before the king of Moab: and they dwelt with him all the while that David was in the hold.

(1 Samuel 22:1–4)

Then they told David, saying, Behold, the Philistines fight against Keilah, and they rob the threshing floors.

Therefore David enquired of the LORD, saying, Shall I go and smite these Philistines? And the LORD said unto David, Go, and smite the Philistines, and save Keilah.

And David's men said unto him, Behold, we be afraid here in Judah: how much more then if we come to Keilah against the armies of the Philistines?

Then David enquired of the Lord yet again. And the Lord answered him and said, Arise, go down to Keilah; for I will deliver the Philistines into thine hand.

So David and his men went to Keilah, and fought with the Philistines, and brought away their cattle, and smote them with a great slaughter. So David saved the inhabitants of Keilah.

(1 Samuel 23:1–5)

———⬥⬥⬥———

t is really interesting to see the kinds of people that God allowed to align themselves with David as he took refuge in the cage. Yes, He sent David's family to dwell with him, but he also sent society's undesirables— those in debt, those depressed, and those in trouble. God sent those people for David to be a captain and a ruler over them. Not only were these men society's undesirables, they were also cowards whom God had appointed to go up against the mighty Philistine army. The men discounted themselves, knowing that they did not have in themselves what it would take to defeat such a valiant and well-established army. I'm sure that had the Philistine army known their back story, they, too, would have laughed at and mocked David's incompetent, cowardly army.

God truly uses the foolish things of the world to confound the wise. He proved to David, and to us, that deliverance is not by the power and might of man, but by the Spirit of God. This same brilliant display of God's power can be found in Judges 7, where God reduced Gideon's army from over thirty thousand to three hundred men, and was explicit in His reasoning: He did not want Israel to take credit for their victory.

God can set us up for huge victories and brilliant displays of His power by taking us low or reducing us. Many times, the world discounts us, and we, acutely aware of our own inadequacies, discount and limit ourselves. We often forget that if God is our source, then we are in the majority. We often forget that greater is He that is in us than He that is in the world (1 John 4:4). But it behooves us to remember that we can do all things through Christ who strengthens us (Philippians 4:13). So when insecurities make an appearance and fear grips us, we must send a clear message that we are not depending on our own strength, but on the strength and power of our omnipotent God. As children of God, one thing we must always keep in mind is that it is all about the glory of God.

Prayer: Father in Heaven, I thank you that you can use me in spite of the many ways that I do not qualify. I break the stronghold of insecurity over my life. I take my focus off myself and fix my eyes on you and on all the ways that you are able. I am so grateful that you are my source and my strength, because your power and might are unlimited. Amen.

The Ways of God (2):

A Message to Our Fears

1 Samuel 22:6–19

When Saul heard that David was discovered, and the men that were with him, (now Saul abode in Gibeah under a tree in Ramah, having his spear in his hand, and all his servants were standing about him;) Then Saul said unto his servants that stood about him, Hear now, ye Benjamites; will the son of Jesse give every one of you fields and vineyards, and make you all captains of thousands, and captains of hundreds; That all of you have conspired against me, and there is none that sheweth me that my son hath made a league with the son of Jesse, and there is none of you that is sorry for me, or sheweth unto me that my son hath stirred up my servant against me, to lie in wait, as at this day?

Then answered Doeg the Edomite, which was set over the servants of Saul, and said, I saw the son of Jesse coming to Nob, to Ahimelech the son of Ahitub. And he enquired of the LORD for him, and gave him victuals, and gave him the sword of Goliath the Philistine. Then the king sent to call Ahimelech the priest, the son of Ahitub, and all his father's house, the priests that were in Nob: and they came all of them to the king. And Saul said, Hear now, thou son of Ahitub. And he answered, Here I am, my lord. And Saul said unto him, Why have ye conspired against me, thou and the son of Jesse, in that thou hast given him bread, and a sword, and hast enquired of God for him, that he should rise against me, to lie in wait, as at this day? Then Ahimelech answered the king, and said, And who is so faithful among all thy servants as David, which is the king's son in law, and goeth at thy bidding, and is honourable in thine house?

Did I then begin to enquire of God for him? be it far from me: let not the king impute any thing unto his servant, nor to all the house of my father: for thy servant knew nothing of all this, less or more. And the king said, Thou shalt surely die, Ahimelech, thou, and all thy father's house. And the king said unto the footmen that stood about him, Turn, and slay the priests of the LORD: because their hand also is with David, and because they knew when he fled, and did not shew it to me. But the servants of the king would not put forth their hand to fall upon the priests of the LORD.

And the king said to Doeg, Turn thou, and fall upon the priests. And Doeg the Edomite turned, and he fell upon the priests, and slew on that day fourscore and five persons that did wear a linen ephod. And Nob, the city of the priests, smote he with the edge of the sword, both men and women, children and sucklings, and oxen, and asses, and sheep, with the edge of the sword.

(1 Samuel 22:6–19)

S aul's paranoia about everyone conspiring against him was a clear sign that God was not his refuge, and that the Spirit of God had left him. Because if God was his refuge, whatever people might have tried to do to him would not have been of grave concern to him.

Fear is like an insidious infection that spreads rapidly and has devastating consequences. Fear often causes us to detour from God-ordained paths. Detouring from the path of trusting God, because of fear, will inevitably lead to us missing out on God's plans and our destiny. Fear is sinister in the things it will cause us to do. Fear was at the root of Saul's appalling decision to kill the priests of the Lord.

The way of God is a life of peace. He is called Jehovah Shalom in Judges 6:24. The depth of peace God gives to us, His children, is profoundly captured in John 14:27, which says, *"Peace I leave with you; my peace I give to you. Not as the world gives do I give to you. Let not your hearts be troubled, neither let them be afraid."* Anxiety, fear, and paranoia are not of God, and reflect a heart that is not meditating on the Word of God. Certainly, in life things arise to rob us of the peace that Christ has given us, and to cause us to be anxious and fearful. David experienced this acutely. The most powerful man in the kingdom of Israel had issued a death warrant, and was obsessed with his obliteration. Yet David's dependence on the God of peace comes through in Psalm 27:1a, as he declared, *"The Lord is my light and my salvation, whom shall I fear?"*

Peace in the midst of turmoil is the way of God. However, dependence on Him is the only way we can have and maintain this peace. When we find ourselves anxious, overwhelmed, or fearful, we need to examine our assumptions and be honest about where we are looking for deliverance. The arm of flesh *will* fail you (Jeremiah 17:5), so if that is your source, fear is logical. But if God is your means of deliverance, and He cannot fail, then accept the peace He gives.

Prayer: Lord, help me to know and understand your ways. Let me not live a life of fear, but learn to trust in you with all of my heart. Father, when circumstances that invoke fear surface in my life, help me to remember that you are my source and that your grace is sufficient for me, in Jesus' name. Amen.

Jehovah Nissi:
The Lord My Banner

1 Samuel 23:6–28

And it came to pass, when Abiathar the son of Ahimelech fled to David to Keilah, that he came down with an ephod in his hand. And it was told Saul that David was come to Keilah. And Saul said, God hath delivered him into mine hand; for he is shut in, by entering into a town that hath gates and bars. And Saul called all the people together to war, to go down to Keilah, to besiege David and his men. And David knew that Saul secretly practised mischief against him; and he said to Abiathar the priest, Bring hither the ephod. Then said David, O LORD God of Israel, thy servant hath certainly heard that Saul seeketh to come to Keilah, to destroy the city for my sake.

Will the men of Keilah deliver me up into his hand? will Saul come down, as thy servant hath heard? O LORD God of Israel, I beseech thee, tell thy servant. And the LORD said, He will come down.

Then said David, Will the men of Keilah deliver me and my men into the hand of Saul? And the LORD said, They will deliver thee up.

Then David and his men, which were about six hundred, arose and departed out of Keilah, and went whithersoever they could go. And it was told Saul that David was escaped from Keilah; and he forbare to go forth. And David abode in the wilderness in strong holds, and remained in a mountain in the wilderness of Ziph. And Saul sought him every day, but God delivered him not into his hand. And David saw that Saul was come out to seek his life: and David was in the wilderness of Ziph in a wood. And Jonathan Saul's son arose, and went to David into the wood, and strengthened his hand in God. And he said unto him, Fear not: for the hand of Saul my father shall not find thee; and thou shalt be king over Israel, and I shall be next unto thee; and that also Saul my father knoweth. And they two made a covenant before the LORD: and David abode in the wood, and Jonathan went to his house.

Then came up the Ziphites to Saul to Gibeah, saying, Doth not David hide himself with us in strong holds in the wood, in the hill of Hachilah, which is on the south of Jeshimon? Now therefore, O king, come down according to all the desire of thy soul to come down; and our part shall be to deliver him into the king's hand.

And Saul said, Blessed be ye of the LORD; for ye have compassion on me.

Go, I pray you, prepare yet, and know and see his place where his haunt is, and who hath seen him there: for it is told me that he dealeth very subtilly.

See therefore, and take knowledge of all the lurking places where he hideth himself, and come ye again to me with the certainty, and I will go with you: and it shall come to pass, if he be in the land, that I will search him out throughout all the thousands of Judah. And they arose, and went to Ziph before Saul: but David and his men were in the wilderness of Maon, in the plain on the south of Jeshimon.

Saul also and his men went to seek him. And they told

David; wherefore he came down into a rock, and abode in the wilderness of Maon. And when Saul heard that, he pursued after David in the wilderness of Maon And Saul went on this side of the mountain, and David and his men on that side of the mountain: and David made haste to get away for fear of Saul; for Saul and his men compassed David and his men round about to take them.

But there came a messenger unto Saul, saying, Haste thee, and come; for the Philistines have invaded the land.

Wherefore Saul returned from pursuing after David, and went against the Philistines: therefore they called that place Selahammahlekoth.

(1 Samuel 23:6–28)

———⬦⬦⬦———

It is almost unimaginable to have someone latch on to you with the sole purpose of destroying you. David had to learn to depend on God, because there was always someone willing to give him up to Saul. God taught him how to dwell in fortresses that He had provided and where He would deliver him. Saul could not touch David, unless God allowed him to. No matter how many leads Saul got or how many people were working with him, David always seemed to evade him. God was a covering for David and a banner from his enemy.

Satan relentlessly seeks to destroy us, just like Saul sought to destroy David. However, the enemy cannot touch us, unless God allows him to, because God is our banner and shield from the enemy. What awesome knowledge it is that God will protect and shield us from the enemy's relentless pursuit to destroy us. Many times, we face situations where our reputations, lives, loved-ones are under attack, and it seems like we have no one on our side as strong or influential as those fighting against us. Such situations are actually ideal for ensuring that our trust and dependence are in Jehovah Nissi. For God will cover those who put their trust in Him, so the enemy cannot get to them to destroy them. The banner of God is impenetrable and a sure place of security. Regardless of how strong the opposition is against us, or how prolonged, Jehovah Nissi will provide hiding places, and grant unto His children ways of escape. We must stay under the banner of God and trust His delivering power and divine protection.

Prayer: Dear God, thank you for your protection against the attacks of the enemy. Please continue to build a hedge around me, and be my banner. Give me peace, knowing that the enemy is unable to destroy me, because he would first have to go through my banner, Jehovah Nissi. Amen.

Strategies of Destruction

1 Samuel 24:1–3 & 26:1–3

And it came to pass, when Saul was returned from following the Philistines, that it was told him, saying, Behold, David is in the wilderness of Engedi.

Then Saul took three thousand chosen men out of all Israel, and went to seek David and his men upon the rocks of the wild goats.

And he came to the sheepcotes by the way, where was a cave; and Saul went in to cover his feet: and David and his men remained in the sides of the cave.

(1 Samuel 24:1–3)

And the Ziphites came unto Saul to Gibeah, saying, Doth not David hide himself in the hill of Hachilah, which is before Jeshimon?

Then Saul arose, and went down to the wilderness of Ziph, having three thousand chosen men of Israel with him, to seek David in the wilderness of Ziph.

And Saul pitched in the hill of Hachilah, which is before Jeshimon, by the way. But David abode in the wilderness, and he saw that Saul came after him into the wilderness.

(1 Samuel 26:1–3)

———⸻———

Whenever Satan wants to destroy you, he becomes hell-bent on tormenting you. Saul was consistently told where David was, and was given updates so that he could not rest from his obsession to haunt and kill David. Leaving the palatial dwelling of a king to prowl around on rocks with wild goats and sleep in caves, with the sole purpose of destroying someone else, is nothing but torture and torment.

So, too, do anger, hatred, jealousy, malice, grudges, resentment, and unforgiveness bring torment and torture. They rob us. It is easy to see why those things are not of God. He gives peace and rest, while they consistently rob us of peace and rest. One thing we must all learn is how to "let it go." For one reason or another, whether we are right or wrong, something will mar a relationship or an acquaintance, and will leave us feeling slighted, hurt, angry, or wronged. At this point, we have a choice in the matter, we can either deal with it and let it go, or hold on to it and torment our souls. It does, in fact, take significant amounts of energy to dislike someone, or to hold on to anger, unforgiveness, and other ill feelings. Of even greater consequence is the fact that we cannot prevent such emotions from infiltrating and hurting our spiritual lives (1 John 4:20; Matthew 6:14–15). Many people have abandoned their families, or walked out of churches and relationship with God because of soured relationships that they have allowed to torment them.

A wise person once said, "Holding on to anger, resentment, or unforgiveness is like drinking poison and expecting the other person to die." Satan uses this tactic to destroy many families, individuals, and churches. We must recognize that *"We wrestle not against flesh and blood, but against principalities, against powers, against the rulers of the darkness of this world, against spiritual wickedness in high places"* (Ephesians 6:12). Until we do, individuals, families, churches, and groups of all types will continue to be tormented. The individual is not the problem, the spirit assigned to bring separation and torment and, ultimately, destroy you is. God's will is for us to walk in love and have peace; the will of our enemy is to bring about division, torment, and destruction.

Prayer: Father in Heaven, I thank you today for opening my eyes to see the strategy of the enemy. I pray for grace to forgive, to let go, and to say, "I'm sorry." When the spirit of division and torment comes, help me to recognize the real enemy and continue to walk in love and peace. Amen,

Responding to Strategies of Destruction:

Overcoming Evil with Good

1 Samuel 24:4–22 & 26:9

And the men of David said unto him, Behold the day of which the LORD said unto thee, Behold, I will deliver thine enemy into thine hand, that thou mayest do to him as it shall seem good unto thee. Then David arose, and cut off the skirt of Saul's robe privily. And it came to pass afterward, that David's heart smote him, because he had cut off Saul's skirt. And he said unto his men, The LORD forbid that I should do this thing unto my master, the LORD's anointed, to stretch forth mine hand against him, seeing he is the anointed of the LORD.

So David stayed his servants with these words, and suffered them not to rise against Saul. But Saul rose up out of the cave, and went on his way. David also arose afterward, and went out of the cave, and cried after Saul, saying, My lord the king. And when Saul looked behind him, David stooped with his face to the earth, and bowed himself. And David said to Saul, Wherefore hearest thou men's words, saying, Behold, David seeketh thy hurt? Behold, this day thine eyes have seen how that the LORD had delivered thee to day into mine hand in the cave: and some bade me kill thee: but mine eye spared thee; and I said, I will not put forth mine hand against my lord;

for he is the LORD's anointed. Moreover, my father, see, yea, see the skirt of thy robe in my hand: for in that I cut off the skirt of thy robe, and killed thee not, know thou and see that there is neither evil nor transgression in mine hand, and I have not sinned against thee; yet thou huntest my soul to take it. The LORD judge between me and thee, and the LORD avenge me of thee: but mine hand shall not be upon thee. As saith the proverb of the ancients, Wickedness proceedeth from the wicked: but mine hand shall not be upon thee. After whom is the king of Israel come out? after whom dost thou pursue? after a dead dog, after a flea. The LORD therefore be judge, and judge between me and thee, and see, and plead my cause, and deliver me out of thine hand.

And it came to pass, when David had made an end of speaking these words unto Saul, that Saul said, Is this thy voice, my son David? And Saul lifted up his voice, and wept. And he said to David, Thou art more righteous than I: for thou hast rewarded me good, whereas I have rewarded thee evil. And thou hast shewed this day how that thou hast dealt well with me: forasmuch as when the LORD had delivered me into thine hand, thou killedst me not. For if a man find his enemy, will he let him go well away? wherefore the LORD reward thee good for that thou hast done unto me this day. And now, behold, I know well that thou shalt surely be king, and that the kingdom of Israel shall be established in thine hand.

Swear now therefore unto me by the LORD, that thou wilt not cut off my seed after me, and that thou wilt not destroy my name out of my father's house. *And David sware unto Saul. And Saul went home; but David and his men gat them up unto the hold.*

(1 Samuel 24:4–22)

And David said to Abishai, Destroy him not: for who can stretch forth his hand against the LORD's anointed, and be guiltless?

(1 Samuel 26:9)

—⊰⊗⊗⊗⊱—

S atan tried to play the same game of torment on David that he played on Saul by telling him where Saul was. He even insinuated that it was God's will for David to allow bitterness and hatred to manifest themselves through him by taking revenge on Saul. Unlike Saul, David did not use the news to try to kill his enemy. Destroying the one who is relentless in their pursuit to destroy you is completely justifiable, and even commonsensical, when engaging in warfare. Instead, David responded in a way that confounded every expectation and, in my estimation, surpassed honour. He used it as an opportunity to show Saul that he was his loyal servant and still regarded him as king and lord. He refused to kill his "master, the Lord's anointed." Although David knew full well that Saul was in the wrong and was not in the will of God, he bowed before his enemy and gave him the honour and respect due to an honourable king.

I love David's humility. He had nothing to prove to anyone. David could have killed Saul, or at least maimed him in order to gloat and to show that he had the upper hand. David could have done it at least to appease his followers or to make them think more highly of him, or to prove himself as a mighty man of valour. He could have done it because Saul had betrayed him multiple times, but he did not. And the little he did, in cutting a piece of his coat, he regretted. David had no qualms about bowing his face to the ground before the appointed king, in a show of subjection and humility.

No matter how justified we would be, or how gratifying it would be, we must remember that vengeance belongs to God, and that He will repay. We ought to stand still and allow God to fight our battles, and remain humble, even when we are being persecuted without cause. David overcame evil with good. David repaid Saul's evil with good. It is the good David did that caused Saul to repent of, and be remorseful about, his evil ways—although short lived—and to speak the blessings of God upon David's life. He admitted to the integrity and righteousness of David.

We, too, must overcome evil with good. We must do good to them that persecute us. It is the good we do to those that hurt us that separates us from the world's standards and speaks as a loud witness to onlookers. When the world sees us loving and forgiving and repaying with good the evil we have received, they are seeing the Christ in us, and may, like Saul, repent and acknowledge our Lord as God.

Prayer: Lord, it is not easy, but your grace is sufficient for me. Help me to overcome evil with good. Give me a heart that is slow to offense, loves easily, forgives quickly, and bears no record of wrong. Let me look to you to justify me and fight my battles. Amen.

Let God Fight Your Battles

1 Samuel 25:39

And when David heard that Nabal was dead, he said, Blessed be the LORD, that hath pleaded the cause of my reproach from the hand of Nabal, and hath kept his servant from evil: for the LORD hath returned the wickedness of Nabal upon his own head. And David sent and communed with Abigail, to take her to him to wife.

(1 Samuel 25:39)

⸺❖⸺

At some point in life, we have all been, and will be, wronged, offended, and unfairly treated. It is inevitable. We live, at least in theory, with a sense of justice, that if we do good unto others, we ought to be repaid with good. Therefore, in times like these, when our notion of fairness is not validated, we feel righteous indignation at what others have done to us, and the desire to avenge ourselves is very strong.

David and his men had been good to Nabal's servants. They had provided protection for Nabal's property and just wanted a little from Nabal's abundance to sustain themselves. At Nabal's refusal, David prepared his men to destroy Nabal and his property, and justifiably so. But God intervened. Sometimes, God's battle plan is for us to stand still and see His salvation (Exodus 14:13). We are not required to fight in our own way, using our own strategies (2 Chronicles 20:17), for vengeance belongs to God (Romans 12:19). Even if we're used to fighting our own way, or God has instructed us with a battle plan that has become our norm, we still ought to take our battles to God. David was used to fighting and destroying, he was a renowned man of war, yet, this time, God's strategy was different. It was for David to just stand still.

God kept David's hand from evil, and fought his battles. David wanted to avenge himself for what he deemed to be injustice done by Nabal. However, God used Abigail to intervene, and then exacted His own justice, not on Nabal's property and servants, which David had planned, but on Nabal himself. God's vengeance was more precise and profound than David's. God did not kill the innocent servants, who had not agreed with their master, but the master himself. In addition, now that David married Abigail, David had access to all that once belonged to Nabal. Had David fought his own battle, he would have destroyed what God wanted to bless him with. The moral of the story: Let God fight your battles.

Prayer: Father, many times I feel wronged and offended, and my anger causes me to want to defend myself. Give me grace, peace, patience, and longsuffering, so that I will take it to you in prayer. Help me not to fight with my own weapons and strategies, but to remember that you will pay and avenge. Give me grace to bless those who curse and despitefully use me, and to leave my battles in your hands, in Jesus' name. Amen.

Inquiring of the Lord:
Too Far to Hear

1 Samuel 28:5–25

And when Saul saw the host of the Philistines, he was afraid, and his heart greatly trembled. And when Saul enquired of the LORD, the LORD answered him not, neither by dreams, nor by Urim, nor by prophets.

Then said Saul unto his servants, Seek me a woman that hath a familiar spirit, that I may go to her, and enquire of her. And his servants said to him, Behold, there is a woman that hath a familiar spirit at Endor.

And Saul disguised himself, and put on other raiment, and he went, and two men with him, and they came to the woman by night: and he said, I pray thee, divine unto me by the familiar spirit, and bring me him up, whom I shall name unto thee.

And the woman said unto him, Behold, thou knowest what Saul hath done, how he hath cut off those that have familiar spirits, and the wizards, out of the land: wherefore then layest thou a snare for my life, to cause me to die? And Saul sware to her by the LORD, saying, As the LORD liveth, there shall no punishment happen to thee for this thing.

Then said the woman, Whom shall I bring up unto thee? And he said, Bring me up Samuel.

And when the woman saw Samuel, she cried with a loud voice: and the woman spake to Saul, saying, Why hast thou deceived me? for thou art Saul.

And the king said unto her, Be not afraid: for what sawest thou? And the woman said unto Saul, I saw gods ascending out of the earth.

And he said unto her, What form is he of? And she said, An old man cometh up; and he is covered with a mantle. And Saul perceived that it was Samuel, and he stooped with his face to the ground, and bowed himself.

And Samuel said to Saul, Why hast thou disquieted me, to bring me up? And Saul answered, I am sore distressed; for the Philistines make war against me, and God is departed from me, and answereth me no more, neither by prophets, nor by dreams: therefore I have called thee, that thou mayest make known unto me what I shall do.

Then said Samuel, Wherefore then dost thou ask of me, seeing the LORD is departed from thee, and is become thine enemy?

And the LORD hath done to him, as he spake by me: for the LORD hath rent the kingdom out of thine hand, and given it to thy neighbour, even to David: Because thou obeyedst not the voice of the LORD, nor executedst his fierce wrath upon Amalek, therefore hath the LORD done this thing unto thee this day.

Moreover the LORD will also deliver Israel with thee into the hand of the Philistines: and to morrow shalt thou and thy sons be with me: the LORD also shall deliver the host of Israel into the hand of the Philistines.

Then Saul fell straightway all along on the earth, and was

sore afraid, because of the words of Samuel: and there was no strength in him; for he had eaten no bread all the day, nor all the night.

And the woman came unto Saul, and saw that he was sore troubled, and said unto him, Behold, thine handmaid hath obeyed thy voice, and I have put my life in my hand, and have hearkened unto thy words which thou spakest unto me.

Now therefore, I pray thee, hearken thou also unto the voice of thine handmaid, and let me set a morsel of bread before thee; and eat, that thou mayest have strength, when thou goest on thy way.

But he refused, and said, I will not eat. But his servants, together with the woman, compelled him; and he hearkened unto their voice. So he arose from the earth, and sat upon the bed.

And the woman had a fat calf in the house; and she hasted, and killed it, and took flour, and kneaded it, and did bake unleavened bread thereof: and she brought it before Saul, and before his servants; and they did eat. Then they rose up, and went away that night.

(1 Samuel 28:5–25)

───※───

Saul inquired of the Lord and got nothing. Instead of seeking God in every season of his life, Saul sought Him in 1 Samuel 28 only out of desperation and fear. But, alas, he was too far from God; there was no relationship or intimacy. Saul was a proud, disobedient king, with no integrity or fear of God. He had neglected and abandoned God, and it seemed that God had done the same to him. The Word of God explicitly states, *"If you seek Him, He will be found of you, but if you forsake Him, He will cast you off forever"* (1 Chronicles 28:9c). A morally and spiritually depraved Saul had no regard for God or the anointed servants of God. He sought God at his convenience and out of despair. It is no wonder he got no answer from God. It is infinitely worse to inquire of God and not hear anything than to inquire and receive direction you do not like, but know it is His will.

The divine will of God is what Christians should seek before making decisions. It is sad, indeed, when we are too far from God to hear from Him. It is incredibly hard to not hear from God in tough times or before making major decisions. Learning from Saul, the first thing we should do when we hear nothing from God is examine our ways and repent. Granted, Saul had done some atrocious things, not the least of which was killing all the priests. But I am convinced that had he repented earnestly of his sins, God would have forgiven him, and may even have given him a word. Isaiah 55:7 says, *"Let the wicked forsake His ways and the unrighteous man his thoughts; let Him return to the Lord that He may have compassion on him, and to our God for He will abundantly pardon."* God has always been a God of mercy. Countless times had the children of Israel turned their backs on God, felt His wrath, repented, turned back to Him, and experienced His love and grace. Saul would have been no different. Unfortunately, Saul dug himself even deeper in the hole; he had a backup plan completely opposite of seeking God. He consulted a diviner, which is prohibited by Mosaic Law.

How many times do we resort to unsavoury and ungodly

backup plans when we can't hear from God, when He hasn't spoken yet, or when we don't like the answer He gives? We must be prepared to earnestly repent and wait on God for the answer. We must be prepared for answers that are not our favourite, because when it's all said and done, our omniscient Father still knows best. No backup plans.

Prayer: Lord, I pray in the name of Jesus Christ of Nazareth that anything in me, or about me, that drives a wedge, or puts distance, between us would be consumed by the Refiner's fire. I need to be so close to you that I hear you, know your heartbeat, know your will, and feel your presence near. Please do not allow me to live a life of rebellion. For what is life if I cannot hear from the source of my life? Amen.

When He Keeps Us From Battle

1 Samuel 29

Now the Philistines gathered together all their armies to Aphek: and the Israelites pitched by a fountain which is in Jezreel.

And the lords of the Philistines passed on by hundreds, and by thousands: but David and his men passed on in the rereward with Achish.

Then said the princes of the Philistines, What do these Hebrews here? And Achish said unto the princes of the Philistines, Is not this David, the servant of Saul the king of Israel, which hath been with me these days, or these years, and I have found no fault in him since he fell unto me unto this day?

And the princes of the Philistines were wroth with him; and the princes of the Philistines said unto him, Make this fellow return, that he may go again to his place which thou hast appointed him, and let him not go down with us to battle, lest in the battle he be an adversary to us: for wherewith should he reconcile himself unto his master? should it not be with the heads of these men?

Is not this David, of whom they sang one to another in

dances, saying, Saul slew his thousands, and David his ten thousands?

Then Achish called David, and said unto him, Surely, as the LORD liveth, thou hast been upright, and thy going out and thy coming in with me in the host is good in my sight: for I have not found evil in thee since the day of thy coming unto me unto this day: nevertheless the lords favour thee not. Wherefore now return, and go in peace, that thou displease not the lords of the Philistines.

And David said unto Achish, But what have I done? and what hast thou found in thy servant so long as I have been with thee unto this day, that I may not go fight against the enemies of my lord the king?

And Achish answered and said to David, I know that thou art good in my sight, as an angel of God: notwithstanding the princes of the Philistines have said, He shall not go up with us to the battle.

Wherefore now rise up early in the morning with thy master's servants that are come with thee: and as soon as ye be up early in the morning, and have light, depart.

So David and his men rose up early to depart in the morning, to return into the land of the Philistines. And the Philistines went up to Jezreel.

(1 Samuel 29)

❈

Sometimes God does not want us to fight the battle, yet He will give us the victory. God is an incredible deliverer. He makes a way of escape where there seems to be no way. David had a burdensome dilemma: to either fight against his people, the Israelites, whom he loved, or deny the request of the Philistine king who had given him refuge from Saul's deadly pursuit (1 Samuel 28:1–2). How would it look for the future king if he fought against the people he sought to rule, with their long-time enemy? And if he refused, what would the Philistine king's response be, who had gone above and beyond and done good to David? Either decision would mar David and mark him as one who had no integrity. Either way would've been like selling his soul, but betrayal of one party was inevitable. Then God supernaturally intervened and made a way by having the princes of the Philistines refuse David's assistance in the war against Israel, thus maintaining his integrity with both the Israelites and the Philistines.

The lesson here is that we owe no loyalty to the world. We must realize that God uses people in the world to bless us, and allows us to find favour with them. But when it comes to choosing, we are to know where our loyalty lies. Blessings, wealth, and increase come from God. He can, and will, use whoever He pleases to bless us. However, at the end of it all, no matter how good they have been, God is our source, and our affection and loyalty belong to Him.

Whether we feel wronged and deserving of justification for the evils done to us, or we are unsure as to our role in a particular battle, we must remember that when God fights our battles, victory is guaranteed. Whether we are angry or confused, we must let God fight our battles, for they are His, not ours (2 Chronicles 20:15). His strategy may differ wildly from ours, and sometimes it may just be a way of escape.

Prayer: Father, please remind me to look to you when I am faced with battles. Regardless of my position, you are my defender. My help and my victory are in you. Amen.

When Battles Come in Quick Succession

1 Samuel 30:1

And it came to pass, when David and his men were come to Ziklag on the third day, that the Amalekites had invaded the south, and Ziklag, and smitten Ziklag, and burned it with fire.

(1 Samuel 30:1)

───◆◆◆───

David was fresh out of a profound dilemma in which He essentially had to choose between being loyal to the Philistine king, who had saved his life and given him refuge when Saul was hunting him down, or being loyal to his people, the Jews, and betray the king. God miraculously intervened and saved him from that decision. But here he was again. As soon as he got back home, he was in the middle of another battle, another struggle.

Sometimes in life it seems as though as soon as God

delivers you out of one situation, you find yourself in the middle of another one. There are no lengthy respites, or even the chance to breathe a sigh of relief. In these times, we are to take heart. Know that the enemy's goal is to destroy the children of God. The Word of God says that the enemy goes about like a roaring lion seeking whom he may devour (1 Peter 5:8). He is the predator, and we are the prey. However, the fact that the enemy is just "like" a roaring lion, already marks him as a counterfeit and an imposter; he has the guise of something but not the power that comes with it. Compare that with Jesus who *is* the Lion of the tribe of Judah, and ultimately triumphs (Revelation 5:5). We who know the Word can have hope in the delivering power of God, and need not succumb to the attacks of the enemy (Psalm 34:19). We are to ask for grace and strength to stand. We are to be steadfast and unmovable. This too shall pass! Refuse to give up. Be strong in the Lord and in the power of His might. Put on the whole armour of God that you may be able to stand against the wiles, the subtle tricks, of the enemy (Ephesians 6:10–11). Greater is He that is in you than he that is in the world (1 John 4:4).

Ironically, right out of a trial is the best time to get into another. Too often, we tend to forget and let the amazement at the delivering power of God become subdued or lessened. It is harder to muster up the faith necessary to face the present battle if you cannot remember the last one God brought you out of. However, if the battles come in relative succession, the delivering power of God is still fresh in your mind, your faith is in high gear, and you are energized. He has just proven that He is able to save, and He can, and will, do it again. You should take all of your victories from the past and stack them up against what you are facing now. The enemy and afflictions are no match for our omnipotent Father. When situations just keep coming up, remember the trials you have just endured and how the mighty hand of God brought you out. Same God, bigger faith. Be it done unto you according to your faith (Matthew 9:29).

Prayer: Abba Father, your Word says you will never give me more than I can bear. Give me grace, faith, and strength to face every battle. Let despair and discouragement be far from me. May the testimonies of your amazing power to deliver be fresh in my mind, and help me to be strong in you and in the power of your might, in Jesus' name. Amen.

Encouraging Yourself in the Lord

1 Samuel 30:3–6

So David and his men came to the city, and, behold, it was burned with fire; and their wives, and their sons, and their daughters, were taken captives.

Then David and the people that were with him lifted up their voice and wept, until they had no more power to weep.

And David's two wives were taken captives, Ahinoam the Jezreelitess, and Abigail the wife of Nabal the Carmelite.

And David was greatly distressed; for the people spake of stoning him, because the soul of all the people was grieved, every man for his sons and for his daughters: but David encouraged himself in the LORD his God.

(1 Samuel 30:3–6)

L ike all of us at some point, David found himself in the midst of a battle so intense and overwhelming that he wept until he had no power left. What do you do when the enemy has stolen everything worth something in your life? What do you do when you turn around and realize that either slowly and methodically, or suddenly and overwhelmingly, the enemy has plundered, pilfered, and destroyed the things that added value to your life? He has stolen your joy, your peace, your children, your spouse, your family, your finances, your health, your dreams. What do you do after you have prayed and cried until you're drained of energy, and even hope? What do you do when those you expect to understand and offer support blame you for the mess and for the enemy's actions? When condemnation is piling up, and there is not one sympathetic soul or compassionate heart that you can find? The Bible tells us that in the midst of this time of devastation and utter dismay, *"David encouraged himself in the Lord his God"* (v. 6).

What might that have looked like? What would we say to encourage ourselves in the Lord? Where can we turn for encouragement but to the Word of God and to His mighty works in our personal lives? This is what I imagine David saying:

"God, you've brought me through many overwhelming and impossible situations before. I believe you can, and will, do it again. Lord, many are the afflictions of the righteous, but you deliver him out of them all" (Psalm 34:19). "You promised, oh God, not to leave me nor forsake me, and I have never seen the righteous forsaken" (Deuteronomy 31:6; Psalm 37:25). "Why art thou cast down, oh my soul, and why art thou disquieted within me? Hope thou in God! For He is the health of my countenance and my God" (Psalm 42:5, 11; 43:5). "Lord, be my strength! For your strength is made perfect in my time of weakness. I trust you, oh God! You've never given me reason not to trust you, because you've never failed me" (2 Corinthians 12:9)."Lord, your eyes go to and fro the whole earth to show yourself strong on behalf of him whose heart is perfect towards you" (2 Chronicles 16:9). "Lord, you are my fortress (Psalm 18:2), my strong tower (Psalm 61:3), my bridge over troubled water, my comforter (Jeremiah 8:18), my guide (Psalm 48:14), the lifter up of my head" (Psalm 3:3). "I know you love me, Lord. I know you care about my affairs. I trust in you."

For Prayer: Compile your own verses, sayings, and songs to encourage yourself in the Lord when things seem to be falling apart. Say them to soothe and encourage yourself, and build your faith.

God Has Already Made a Way

1 Samuel 30:2, 9–15; 2 Samuel 17:1–14

And had taken the women captives, that were therein: they slew not any, either great or small, but carried them away, and went on their way.

(1 Samuel 30:2)

So David went, he and the six hundred men that were with him, and came to the brook Besor, where those that were left behind stayed.

But David pursued, he and four hundred men: for two hundred abode behind, which were so faint that they could not go over the brook Besor.

And they found an Egyptian in the field, and brought him to David, and gave him bread, and he did eat; and they made him drink water;

And they gave him a piece of a cake of figs, and two clusters of raisins: and when he had eaten, his spirit came again to him: for he had eaten no bread, nor drunk any water, three days and three nights.

And David said unto him, To whom belongest thou? and whence art thou? And he said, I am a young man of Egypt, servant to an Amalekite; and my master left me, because three days agone I fell sick.

We made an invasion upon the south of the Cherethites, and upon the coast which belongeth to Judah, and upon the south of Caleb; and we burned Ziklag with fire.

And David said to him, Canst thou bring me down to this company? And he said, Swear unto me by God, that thou wilt neither kill me, nor deliver me into the hands of my master, and I will bring thee down to this company.

(1 Samuel 30:9–15)

Moreover Ahithophel said unto Absalom, Let me now choose out twelve thousand men, and I will arise and pursue after David this night: And I will come upon him while he is weary and weak handed, and will make him afraid: and all the people that are with him shall flee; and I will smite the king only: And I will bring back all the people unto thee: the man whom thou seekest is as if all returned: so all the people shall be in peace. And the saying pleased Absalom well, and all the elders of Israel.

Then said Absalom, Call now Hushai the Archite also, and let us hear likewise what he saith. And when Hushai was come to Absalom, Absalom spake unto him, saying, Ahithophel hath spoken after this manner: shall we do after his saying? if not; speak thou.

And Hushai said unto Absalom, The counsel that Ahithophel hath given is not good at this time.

For, said Hushai, thou knowest thy father and his men, that they be mighty men, and they be chafed in their minds, as a bear robbed of her whelps in the field: and thy father is a man of war, and will not lodge with the people.

Behold, he is hid now in some pit, or in some other place: and it will come to pass, when some of them be overthrown at the first, that whosoever heareth it will say, There is a slaughter among the people that follow Absalom.

And he also that is valiant, whose heart is as the heart of a lion, shall utterly melt: for all Israel knoweth that thy father is a mighty man, and they which be with him are valiant men.

Therefore I counsel that all Israel be generally gathered unto thee, from Dan even to Beersheba, as the sand that is by the sea for multitude; and that thou go to battle in thine own person.

So shall we come upon him in some place where he shall be found, and we will light upon him as the dew falleth on the ground: and of him and of all the men that are with him there shall not be left so much as one.

Moreover, if he be gotten into a city, then shall all Israel bring ropes to that city, and we will draw it into the river, until there be not one small stone found there.

And Absalom and all the men of Israel said, The counsel of Hushai the Archite is better than the counsel of Ahithophel. For the LORD had appointed to defeat the good counsel of Ahithophel, to the intent that the LORD might bring evil upon Absalom.

(2 Samuel 17:1–14)

————◆◇◆————

When your battle is most intense, do not dismay; God has already made the way to victory. God had so ordained it that the Amalekites would not kill any of the women and children they had taken for spoil, because He had already planned to allow His son to recover all. God had also ordained for the Amalekites to leave that servant out in the field to die so that he would serve as a guide, and lead David and his army to the plunderers. Similarly, in 2 Samuel, while David was in exile because of Absalom, his son, he kept saying that God would restore him, if that was His will. He refused to fight or avenge himself. And how right he was. Even when David was completely oblivious to the plan of his enemy to destroy him, God had already worked out a way to restore David and destroy his enemy (2 Samuel 17:1–14). God would confuse the enemy and cause wise counsel to fail, so as to protect David and his men from attack.

Sometimes in the midst of the battle, all we see is the doom and gloom. In the midst of the storm, all we see are the thick, dark, menacing clouds promising a relentless onslaught of rain. Yet what we fail to see is what is most relevant to us. We fail to see the rainbow that promises reprise because it represents the covenant of God not to destroy the earth by water. We fail to see the intricate, and sometimes secret, ways that God is working things out. We fail to see the roadmap and the foundation that He is laying for our deliverance. In the heat of the battle, we don't often see that God has already made a way and is about to use the enemy's own hands against him. Granted, our mortal eyes can only see so far, and an overwhelmed heart can only hope for so much. In times like these, we must trust in God. Know that He is always fighting on your side, always mapping your deliverance. The way has already been made. There are loopholes in the enemy's tactics and decisions that are there to ensure your deliverance. Do not allow what you can see to discourage you, task your faith, and rob you of your hope. Do not allow the situation to intimidate you, because its defeat is imminent. Rest assured that in due time it will work together for your good. Whatever you focus on will be made bigger and resonate in your spirit. Look past your problem and see the God who is able to solve it. He already knows the exact time of your deliverance and the method by which it will be attained. Although you cannot see it, God has already made the way. We don't have to fight our battles. God has already ordained the way in which you will triumph over your enemy. Even before the fight starts or we know that the enemy is plotting our demise, God ordains our victory.

Prayer: Father in Heaven, please increase my faith. Strengthen me in the time of trouble and let me not give in to despair. Help me to trust in you and to know that my deliverance is all planned out. My help is in you, oh God, and so I hope in you. Thank you for the way of escape, in Jesus' name. Amen.

Know Your Source

1 Samuel 30:21–31

And David came to the two hundred men, which were so faint that they could not follow David, whom they had made also to abide at the brook Besor: and they went forth to meet David, and to meet the people that were with him: and when David came near to the people, he saluted them. Then answered all the wicked men and men of Belial, of those that went with David, and said, Because they went not with us, we will not give them ought of the spoil that we have recovered, save to every man his wife and his children, that they may lead them away, and depart. Then said David, Ye shall not do so, my brethren, with that which the Lord hath given us, who hath preserved us, and delivered the company that came against us into our hand. For who will hearken unto you in this matter? but as his part is that goeth down to the battle, so shall his part be that tarrieth by the stuff: they shall part alike. *And it was so from that day forward, that he made it a statute and an ordinance for Israel unto this day. And when David came to Ziklag, he sent of the spoil unto the elders of Judah, even to his friends, saying, Behold a present for you of the spoil of the enemies of the Lord; To them which were in Bethel, and to them which were in south Ramoth, and to them which were in Jattir, And to them which were in Aroer, and to them which were in Siphmoth, and to them which were in Eshtemoa, And to them which were in Rachal, and to them which were in the cities of the Jerahmeelites, and to them which were in the cities of the Kenites, And to them which were in Hormah, and to them which were in Chorashan, and to them which were in Athach, And to them which were in Hebron, and to all the places where David himself and his men were wont to haunt.*

(1 Samuel 30:21–31)

---

t is a notable lesson that after David returned from battle with all the spoil, he did not shun those men who could not make it to the battle, but shared the spoil with them. When the men who did fight the battle were angered by this decision, David indirectly revealed the reason for his actions: He knew his source. He said, *"You shall not do so my brethren with that which <u>the Lord hath given to us</u>"* (v. 23). Unlike his followers, David did not think that the recovery of the spoil and the victory in the battle were as a result of his own might and prowess and valour (Psalm 33:16–17). He knew that the Lord his God had mercifully allowed them to recover what the enemy had stolen. So, in like manner, David chose to mercifully bestow equal shares upon the men who could not make it into battle, and send to his friends and allies everywhere.

There is something profound about knowing our source. It keeps us humble and makes us compassionate towards others. If we know that our victories and successes are the direct result of the divine intervention of God, then we cannot become puffed up with pride. When we recognize our source, we do not look down on others. We are eager to be unto others as Christ has been unto us. It is true that the men were too weak and, quite frankly, incompetent to go and fight, and probably did not deserve an equal share of the spoil. However, honest reflection of our own lives will reveal our own unworthiness. Grace, by definition, is "the love and mercy given to us by God, because God desires us to have it, not because of anything we have done to earn it" (www.umc. org). Grace is a gift, not a reward from God.

Are there undeserving people in your life that you are waiting to "come up to par" to earn certain things from you? Remember all that God has given you in spite of your own shortcomings. The more we recognize that our lives are a result of the grace, mercy, and blessings of God, and not of our own doing, the more we want to be a blessing to others. Know your source.

Prayer: Father in Heaven, I thank you for your blessings. Please help me to always reflect on your grace. As a sign of gratitude to you, may I in turn show grace to others. Teach me how to be kind, compassionate, and understanding, how to give when it is not earned or deserved. Help me to be humble in my accomplishments, knowing that you are the source of it all.

To Be a Blessing

2 Samuel 7:1–3

And it came to pass, when the king sat in his house, and the LORD had given him rest round about from all his enemies;
That the king said unto Nathan the prophet, See now, I dwell in an house of cedar, but the ark of God dwelleth within curtains.
And Nathan said to the king, Go, do all that is in thine heart; for the LORD is with thee.

(2 Samuel 7:1–3)

David's plan to build a temple for God—although we later find out that it was not God's will—reminds me of our need to be a blessing. God had blessed David. He was finally king over all the children of Israel, and God had given him rest from his enemies. Instead of selfishly absorbing the blessings of God and seeking his continued comfort, David aspired to be a blessing and to do something for God in return. He wasn't satisfied with just being blessed.

As children of God, we are blessed, and like David, we are to aspire to be a blessing to others. Firstly, we are to be a blessing to God and the Kingdom of God. The elaborate displays of God's faithfulness in our lives should inspire us to walk closer with Him and surrender ourselves more fully to Him. Psalm 116:12–13 says poignantly, *"What shall I render unto the Lord for all His benefits towards me? I will take up the cup of salvation and call upon the name of the Lord."* The most impressive way to tell God thanks for His love and all that He has done is to give Him all that we are in return. The well-known Easter hymn by Isaac Watts says, "Love so amazing [and] so divine, demands my soul, my life, my all."

Secondly, we are to be a blessing to others. There are always needs that we can meet, always something we can do to make someone else's life easier. The Bible talks about the widows and the orphans, and the Word says, *"He that giveth to the poor lendeth to God"* (Proverbs 19:17). There are many ways to be a blessing; it doesn't always include money, it can be out of whatever God has blessed you with. Let us not sit back on God's blessings. Let us pass it on or pay it forward, for God has been good to us.

Prayer: Father, in Jesus' name, help me to be a blessing. Open my eyes and heart that I may see and tend to the needs of others. Amen.

To Turn and Live, or to Stay and Die

1 Samuel 31

Now the Philistines fought against Israel: and the men of Israel fled from before the Philistines, and fell down slain in mount Gilboa. And the Philistines followed hard upon Saul and upon his sons; and the Philistines slew Jonathan, and Abinadab, and Melchishua, Saul's sons. And the battle went sore against Saul, and the archers hit him; and he was sore wounded of the archers. Then said Saul unto his armourbearer, Draw thy sword, and thrust me through therewith; lest these uncircumcised come and thrust me through, and abuse me. But his armourbearer would not; for he was sore afraid. Therefore Saul took a sword, and fell upon it. And when his armourbearer saw that Saul was dead, he fell likewise upon his sword, and died with him. So Saul died, and his three sons, and his armourbearer, and all his men, that same day together.

And when the men of Israel that were on the other side of the valley, and they that were on the other side Jordan, saw that the men of Israel fled, and that Saul and his sons were dead, they forsook the cities, and fled; and the Philistines came and dwelt in them. And it came to pass on the morrow, when the Philistines came to strip the slain, that they found Saul and his three sons fallen in mount Gilboa. And they cut off his head, and stripped off his armour, and sent into the land of the Philistines round about, to publish it in the house of their idols, and among the people. And they put his armour in the house of Ashtaroth: and they fastened his body to the wall of Bethshan. And when the inhabitants of Jabeshgilead heard of that which the Philistines had done to Saul; All the valiant men arose, and went all night, and took the body of Saul and the bodies of his sons from the wall of Bethshan, and came to Jabesh, and burnt them there. And they took their bones, and buried them under a tree at Jabesh, and fasted seven days.

(1 Samuel 31)

S aul's ending was indeed a sad one. How did this valiant man, who was chosen out of all the Israelite men to be the first king of Israel, because he was more impressive than all, in stature and looks, end up taking his own life and dying such a pitiful death? Saul, like many Christians, started well, and at no point did he overtly and decisively decide to stop following God. What Saul did was allow the little schemes of the enemy to work in his life—a little disobedience that he could justify, a little jealousy he let fester and blossom in his heart, and a little pride and stubbornness. In the season before he died, Saul was far from God, and he knew it. He had messed up, and I am sure he realized his folly. However, now that the enemy had robbed and disgraced him, he wanted to kill him and finish the job so that there would be no chance of return.

How many times do we, as children of God, backslide or mess up and find ourselves where Saul was towards the end of his life? Wounded, but not dead; disgraced, with everything around us lost, because we lost our connection with God. I firmly believe that it is never too late to make things right with God. Saul had been badly wounded by the enemy's arrows, and was in a pitiful position, but he still had life; hence, he had a chance to repent.

God is an awesome God of mercy, and it is not His will for anyone to perish. Saul could have turned and lived. But like he does with many of us, Lucifer, the enemy of our souls, undoubtedly filled Saul with condemnation and convinced him that he had gone too far from God. Saul listened to the enemy's lies and chose to stay in his folly and die a pitiful and pathetic death. He started well, messed up, could have turned, but instead stayed and died. Do not be like Saul. Do not stay and die. The grace of God can reach you wherever you are. He does not love you any less because you have messed up. Like the father of the prodigal son in Luke 15:11–32, God is waiting for you to return. He will rejoice and throw a huge party in your honour upon your return. Yes, you have eaten some pig's food; yes, you are wounded, but you do not have to stay there, God is waiting to welcome you home, back into His fold. To turn and live or stay and die, the choice is yours.

Prayer: Heavenly Father, I thank you for grace. I bless you that you are a God of numerous chances. Examine me today, and forgive me of my sins. I acknowledge my transgressions, oh Lord, blot them out I pray. I want to return to the fold to live in your divine will and fullness. Help me to renounce sin and walk in obedience to you in all things. Thank you for taking me back, and for grace to please you with my life. Amen.

Bearing with the Failings of the Weak

2 Samuel 1

Now it came to pass after the death of Saul, when David was returned from the slaughter of the Amalekites, and David had abode two days in Ziklag; It came even to pass on the third day, that, behold, a man came out of the camp from Saul with his clothes rent, and earth upon his head: and so it was, when he came to David, that he fell to the earth, and did obeisance. And David said unto him, From whence comest thou? And he said unto him, Out of the camp of Israel am I escaped. And David said unto him, How went the matter? I pray thee, tell me. And he answered, That the people are fled from the battle, and many of the people also are fallen and dead; and Saul and Jonathan his son are dead also. And David said unto the young man that told him, How knowest thou that Saul and Jonathan his son be dead? And the young man that told him said, As I happened by chance upon mount Gilboa, behold, Saul leaned upon his spear; and, lo, the chariots and horsemen followed hard after him. And when he looked behind him, he saw me, and called unto me. And I answered, Here am I. And he said unto me, Who art thou? And I answered him, I am an

Amalekite. He said unto me again, Stand, I pray thee, upon me, and slay me: for anguish is come upon me, because my life is yet whole in me. So I stood upon him, and slew him, because I was sure that he could not live after that he was fallen: and I took the crown that was upon his head, and the bracelet that was on his arm, and have brought them hither unto my lord. Then David took hold on his clothes, and rent them; and likewise all the men that were with him: And they mourned, and wept, and fasted until even, for Saul, and for Jonathan his son, and for the people of the LORD, and for the house of Israel; because they were fallen by the sword. And David said unto the young man that told him, Whence art thou? And he answered, I am the son of a stranger, an Amalekite. And David said unto him, How wast thou not afraid to stretch forth thine hand to destroy the LORD's anointed? And David called one of the young men, and said, Go near, and fall upon him. And he smote him that he died. And David said unto him, Thy blood be upon thy head; for thy mouth hath testified against thee, saying, I have slain the LORD's anointed. And David lamented with this lamentation over Saul and over Jonathan his son: (Also he bade them teach the children of Judah the use of the bow: behold, it is written in the book of Jasher.) The beauty of Israel is slain upon thy high places: how are the mighty fallen! Tell it not in Gath, publish it not in the streets of Askelon; lest the daughters of the Philistines rejoice, lest the daughters of the uncircumcised triumph. Ye mountains of Gilboa, let there be no dew, neither let there be rain, upon you, nor fields of offerings: for there the shield of the mighty is vilely cast away, the shield of Saul, as though he had not been anointed with oil. From the blood of the slain, from the fat of the mighty, the bow of Jonathan turned not back, and the sword of Saul returned not empty. Saul and Jonathan were lovely and pleasant in *their lives, and in their death they were not divided: they were swifter than eagles, they were stronger than lions. Ye daughters of Israel, weep over Saul, who clothed you in scarlet, with other delights, who put on ornaments of gold upon your apparel. How are the mighty fallen in the midst of the battle! O Jonathan, thou wast slain in thine high places. I am distressed for thee, my brother Jonathan: very pleasant hast thou been unto me: thy love to me was wonderful, passing the love of women. How are the mighty fallen, and the weapons of war perished!*

(2 Samuel 1)

E ven after all Saul had done, David still respected and honoured him as God's anointed. David did not take his death lightly, nor did he rejoice over it. He did not agree with the messenger that finishing the king was the right thing to do. David did not share the notion that, just because the king had fallen by his own doings, it was okay to finish destroying him. Instead, righteous indignation and utter disgust rose up in David at what the young man, regardless of his motives, had claimed to have done to the man whom God had appointed and anointed as king. Then he heart-wrenchingly and sincerely mourned and lamented and prayed. He wished that he could cover it all up so the enemies would not hear and rejoice, and he encouraged the people to remember the good their king had done for them.

In our world today, we hear a lot about men and women of God in high office, and even church members falling and doing things that are detrimental to themselves, their ministries, and the church of God. In times like these, the world and the media and even other believers have a field day with the salacious stories and the scandalous gossip. We discuss the events with believers and unbelievers alike, criticizing, denouncing, and demeaning not just the action but also the person. Most times we feel completely justified in our self-righteousness and judgement. We conveniently forget scriptures like 1 Peter 5:8, which says, *"The enemy prowls around like a roaring lion seeking someone to devour;"* or 1 Corinthians 10:12, that those who think they stand need to be careful lest they fall; or Romans 15:1, that the strong are to bear with the failings of the weak; or 1 Peter 4:8, that love covers a multitude of sins; or 1 Corinthians 13:7, that love always protects, and believes the best and hopes for the best and endures all things.

Any attack against a believer is the plan of the enemy to discredit and destroy the church, to bring shame and reproach to the gospel and the body of Christ, not just to the fallen individual but to us all. We, as children of God, should never engage lightly in such discussions, and God forbid that we should gossip about and condemn others. A blow to one is a blow to us all; it affects all of our evangelism and our identity as Christians. We must, like David, mourn and lament the situation. We must pray that the enemy's plan to mock the church and rejoice be thwarted. We must be fervent in prayer, stand in the gap, and intercede for the fallen brother or sister, those who might turn away from the gospel because of the story, and for ourselves that we stand and not fall to the cunning deception of the enemy. We must encourage one another to remember the good the person has done, believe the best, and let love cover a multitude of sins. Do not cover-up for sin, but do not rejoice in, disdain, or condemn other believers, even in their shortcomings.

Prayer: Father, please help me to remain vigilant, and keep my feet from falling. Help me to walk in love, forgiveness, and compassion for other believers. Give me wisdom to deal with their shortcomings, and thwart the enemy's plans to destroy the church. Amen.

Promotion Comes from the Lord:

Appointed By Whom?

2 Samuel 2:1–10

And it came to pass after this, that David enquired of the LORD, saying, Shall I go up into any of the cities of Judah? And the LORD said unto him, Go up. And David said, Whither shall I go up? And he said, Unto Hebron.

So David went up thither, and his two wives also, Ahinoam the Jezreelitess, and Abigail Nabal's wife the Carmelite. And his men that were with him did David bring up, every man with his household: and they dwelt in the cities of Hebron. And the men of Judah came, and there they anointed David king over the house of Judah. And they told David, saying, That the men of Jabeshgilead were they that buried Saul. And David sent messengers unto the men of Jabeshgilead, and said unto them, Blessed be ye of the LORD, that ye have shewed this kindness unto your lord, even unto Saul, and have buried him. And now the LORD shew kindness and truth unto you: and I also will requite you this kindness, because ye have done this thing. Therefore now let your hands be strengthened, and be ye valiant: for your master Saul is dead, and also the house of Judah have anointed me king over them. But Abner the son of Ner, captain of Saul's host, took Ishbosheth the son of

Saul, and brought him over to Mahanaim; And made him king over Gilead, and over the Ashurites, and over Jezreel, and over Ephraim, and over Benjamin, and over all Israel. Ishbosheth Saul's son was forty years old when he began to reign over Israel, and reigned two years. But the house of Judah followed David.

(2 Samuel 2:1–10)

I t is interesting how the two men—David and Ishbosheth—were appointed in this chapter. David was appointed by God and physically anointed by Samuel, the priest of God from childhood (see 1 Samuel 16). The chapter begins with David inquiring of the Lord and receiving divine leading to go up into Judah, where he received his second anointing, which only served as a confirmation of what God had already ordained. Ishbosheth, on the other hand, was appointed and made king by Abner, a mere mortal. Nowhere does the Bible mention Ishbosheth's wisdom or valour, or even record his voice, and there is certainly no mention of the will of God. One thing is certain, as per Psalm 75:6–7, promotion does not come from the east nor the west nor the north nor the south, but from God. It is God who exalts one and puts the other down. Undoubtedly, Abner appointed Ishbosheth to be king because of who he was—the son of the late King Saul. In Abner's finite mind, that qualified Ishbosheth to be king. However, David would never have been anointed or appointed to be king if it was left up to Samuel, who was sure that David's oldest brother looked like kingly material and should be chosen, or to his father Jesse, who was so sure David could never be king that he didn't even bother to call him from the field when the priest came to anoint one of his sons to be king.

We must be wary in the church of manmade appointments for our lives. Just because it may be a good thing, or even a necessary thing, does not mean it is God's will for our lives. God gives grace, divine enablement, for us to do the things that *He* wants us to do. The things that we allow others to talk us into, and convince us to do, carry no such grace. When we find ourselves doing things that we were neither appointed nor anointed by God to do, they become unpleasant chores, frustrating, joyless, tedious, and time-consuming. We are to seek the leading of the Holy Spirit, and not blindly yield to the will of man. Just because someone suggests it or thinks it's best for you, or it's logical for you, doesn't mean that God has anointed, appointed, or ordained you for the position. Undoubtedly, we need guidance and leadership, but manmade opinions should not be our deciding factor. Your spirit needs to bear witness to the appointment. Seek the will of God, and that alone. Nothing else will carry grace and be fulfilling.

Prayer: Father in Heaven, please let me be led by the Spirit of God. Show me the paths that you have ordained for me to take. Let me know the difference between your speaking through someone else and a manmade appointment. May I never seek to please others by blindly following their opinions. May the will of God be the way that I take, in Jesus' name. Amen.

Appointment & Compromise

2 Samuel 3:6–11

And it came to pass, while there was war between the house of Saul and the house of David, that Abner made himself strong for the house of Saul.

And Saul had a concubine, whose name was Rizpah, the daughter of Aiah: and Ishbosheth said to Abner, Wherefore hast thou gone in unto my father's concubine?

Then was Abner very wroth for the words of Ishbosheth, and said, Am I a dog's head, which against Judah do shew kindness this day unto the house of Saul thy father, to his brethren, and to his friends, and have not delivered thee into the hand of David, that thou chargest me to day with a fault concerning this woman?

So do God to Abner, and more also, except, as the LORD hath sworn to David, even so I do to him;

To translate the kingdom from the house of Saul, and to set up the throne of David over Israel and over Judah, from Dan even to Beersheba.

And he could not answer Abner a word again, because he feared him.

(2 Samuel 3:6–11)

King Ishbosheth's response to an insubordinate Abner is exactly why we cannot allow people to appoint us to positions or tasks not ordained by God. When our source of power, or claim to positions of authority, comes from people, we tend to fear them and the power they have over us. In contrast, when we are appointed by God, we only seek to please Him, knowing that if God appointed us we will not be moved until He moves us. Abner was sleeping with the deceased king's concubine, which was a huge violation and was as significant as his claiming the throne. However, Ishbosheth, the king, could not stand up to his servant, because he had allowed his servant, and not God, to determine his appointment, when they both knew that David was the God-ordained successor to the throne.

Sometimes Christians, especially those in positions of authority, have more fear for man than they do for God. They compromise their standards and convictions in order to please the people they rule over, as though it were the people who appointed them. Even for Christian politicians there must be an understanding that promotion and demotion come only from our sovereign God, so when we are in places of authority, He is the only one we need to fear. Christian employees compromise to keep their jobs, Christian students compromise to get a good grade, and friends compromise to remain in the circle. Too often, we get so afraid that people will take our position from us that we compromise in an effort to keep it. But in those cases we are completely delusional, because when God sets us up, only He can take us down. And irrespective of how much you compromise, when He says it is time for you to go, no one can keep you in the position. David is an excellent example of this principle. God ordained David to be the king, and regardless of what Saul or Abner did in order to stop it, or all the other logical factors standing in his way, David eventually became king. Why? Because God appointed him to the position. Fear only God, and stand up for righteousness.

Prayer: Father, in the name of Jesus, please help me to fear only you, and recognize you as my source. Help me to not compromise, and give me wisdom to stand up for what is right in your sight. Let others see Christ in me, even if it costs me things I hold dear. Amen.

Promotion & Devious Means

2 Samuel 4:2–12

And Saul's son had two men that were captains of bands: the name of the one was Baanah, and the name of the other Rechab, the sons of Rimmon a Beerothite, of the children of Benjamin: (for Beeroth also was reckoned to Benjamin. And the Beerothites fled to Gittaim, and were sojourners there until this day.)

And Jonathan, Saul's son, had a son that was lame of his feet. He was five years old when the tidings came of Saul and Jonathan out of Jezreel, and his nurse took him up, and fled: and it came to pass, as she made haste to flee, that he fell, and became lame. And his name was Mephibosheth.

And the sons of Rimmon the Beerothite, Rechab and Baanah, went, and came about the heat of the day to the house of Ishbosheth, who lay on a bed at noon.

And they came thither into the midst of the house, as though they would have fetched wheat; and they smote him under the fifth rib: and Rechab and Baanah his brother escaped.

For when they came into the house, he lay on his bed in his bedchamber, and they smote him, and slew him, and beheaded him, and took his head, and gat them away through the plain all night.

And they brought the head of Ishbosheth unto David to Hebron, and said to the king, Behold the head of Ishbosheth the son of Saul thine enemy, which sought thy life; and the LORD hath avenged my lord the king this day of Saul, and of his seed.

And David answered Rechab and Baanah his brother, the sons of Rimmon the Beerothite, and said unto them, As the LORD liveth, who hath redeemed my soul out of all adversity,

When one told me, saying, Behold, Saul is dead, thinking to have brought good tidings, I took hold of him, and slew him in Ziklag, who thought that I would have given him a reward for his tidings:

How much more, when wicked men have slain a righteous person in his own house upon his bed? shall I not therefore now require his blood of your hand, and take you away from the earth?

And David commanded his young men, and they slew them, and cut off their hands and their feet, and hanged them up over the pool in Hebron. But they took the head of Ishbosheth, and buried it in the sepulchre of Abner in Hebron.

(2 Samuel 4:2–12)

---

shbosheth was murdered by people who were in his camp. No doubt they heard of Abner's death and figured that David would soon overthrow Ishbosheth and reign as king. Therefore, in order to gain favour with David, they killed the current king, beheaded him, and took his head to David. These evil and opportunistic men were trying to secure a place for themselves with David; instead, they encountered his wrath and were put to death. Unlike Ishbosheth and the villains who killed him, David knew where his promotion came from. It was God who had appointed him to be king, and who had kept him all these years from the hands of Saul who sought his life. Therefore, he did not require the help of these wicked men who did an evil deed and tried to pass it off as the will of God.

Whenever we fail to understand or recognize God as the source of promotion, we will undoubtedly engage in fleshly attempts to gain appointments. Unfortunately, too often these fleshly attempts to gain promotion result in sinful, deceptive, and sinister plots. Sadly, sometimes we try to use other people's failures, grief, and mishaps as opportunities to advance ourselves. Even worse, we are willing to bring people down in order to get an opportunity to be promoted. Slandering, starting rumours, gossiping, sabotaging, undermining, lying, cheating, scheming, and even remaining silent when someone else is the victim of such attempts at character assassination, when we stand to benefit, are abominable. A lack of remorse for those negatively affected by our ruthless ambitions is often justified by the phrase "collateral damage." But are we not all humans, made of flesh and blood, with emotions and loved ones? Deceit and other sinful means will never get us where we want to be or give us peace. Like David, we have to know our source and understand that a holy God does not require the evil intervention of human beings to achieve His divine plan. Favour and promotion come from God, and if we fail to compromise, and we do what He would have us do, then we will get there and have peace, if it is His divine will.

Prayer: Lord, I come before you as I am, imperfect. Please forgive me for not setting my eyes on you as the source of my promotion, and for any evil I may have engaged in to achieve my desires. Keep me in your divine will, wherever that may lead. You are my God, and your Word promises that you will withhold nothing good from me. Amen.

The Unravelling Effects of Failure to Inquire

2 Samuel 3:12–39

And Abner sent messengers to David on his behalf, saying, Whose is the land? saying also, Make thy league with me, and, behold, my hand shall be with thee, to bring about all Israel unto thee. And he said, Well; I will make a league with thee: but one thing I require of thee, that is, Thou shalt not see my face, except thou first bring Michal Saul's daughter, when thou comest to see my face. And David sent messengers to Ishbosheth Saul's son, saying, Deliver me my wife Michal, which I espoused to me for an hundred foreskins of the Philistines.

And Ishbosheth sent, and took her from her husband, even from Phaltiel the son of Laish. And her husband went with her along weeping behind her to Bahurim. Then said Abner unto him, Go, return. And he returned. And Abner had communication with the elders of Israel, saying, Ye sought for David in times past to be king over you: Now then do it: for the LORD hath spoken of David, saying, By the hand of my servant David I will save my people Israel out of the hand of the Philistines, and out of the hand of all their enemies.

And Abner also spake in the ears of Benjamin: and Abner went also to speak in the ears of David in Hebron all that seemed good to Israel, and that seemed good to the whole house of Benjamin.

So Abner came to David to Hebron, and twenty men with him. And David made Abner and the men that were with him a feast. And Abner said unto David, I will arise and go, and will gather all Israel unto my lord the king, that they may make a league with thee, and that thou mayest reign over all that thine heart desireth. And David sent Abner away; and he went in peace.

And, behold, the servants of David and Joab came from pursuing a troop, and brought in a great spoil with them: but Abner was not with David in Hebron; for he had sent him away, and he was gone in peace.

When Joab and all the host that was with him were come, they told Joab, saying, Abner the son of Ner came to the king, and he hath sent him away, and he is gone in peace.

Then Joab came to the king, and said, What hast thou done? behold, Abner came unto thee; why is it that thou hast sent him away, and he is quite gone? Thou knowest Abner the son of Ner, that he came to deceive thee, and to know thy going out and thy coming in, and to know all that thou doest. And when Joab was come out from David, he sent messengers after Abner, which brought him again from the well of Sirah: but David knew it not. And when Abner was returned to Hebron, Joab took him aside in the gate to speak with him quietly, and smote him there under the fifth rib, that he died, for the blood of Asahel his brother. And afterward when David heard it, he said, I and my kingdom are guiltless before the LORD for ever from the blood of Abner the son of Ner: Let it rest on the head of Joab, and on all his father's house; and let there not fail from the house of Joab one that hath an issue, or that is a leper, or that leaneth on a staff, or that falleth on the sword, or that lacketh bread.

So Joab, and Abishai his brother slew Abner, because he had slain their brother Asahel at Gibeon in the battle.

And David said to Joab, and to all the people that were with him, Rend your clothes, and gird you with sackcloth, and mourn before Abner. And king David himself followed the bier. And they buried Abner in Hebron: and the king lifted up his voice, and wept at the grave of Abner; and all the people wept. And the king lamented over Abner, and said, Died Abner as a fool dieth? Thy hands were not bound, nor thy feet put into fetters: as a man falleth before wicked men, so fellest thou. And all the people wept again over him. And when all the people came to cause David to eat meat while it was yet day, David sware, saying, So do God to me, and more also, if I taste bread, or ought else, till the sun be down. And all the people took notice of it, and it pleased them: as whatsoever the king did pleased all the people. For all the people and all Israel understood that day that it was not of the king to slay Abner the son of Ner.

And the king said unto his servants, Know ye not that there is a prince and a great man fallen this day in Israel? And I am this day weak, though anointed king; and these men the sons of Zeruiah be too hard for me: the LORD shall reward the doer of evil according to his wickedness.

(2 Samuel 3:12–39)

The league between David and Abner was unsettling from its onset. Yet the biggest failure here was a glaring omission. David did not inquire of the Lord as to how to proceed with Abner's request for a covenant. Had the king of Judah inquired of the Lord, he would have known that Abner was a scheming and non-submissive servant, who was only seeking an alliance because the king of Israel had attempted to correct him. The same way Abner took it upon himself to establish Ishbosheth as king of Israel, which made the king afraid to reprove him, was the way he wanted to help appoint David, as if it were his duty to appoint kings based on his whim. How did David know, given Abner's traitorous and treacherous background, that Abner would not do the same thing to him when he was dissatisfied or had some other motive?

This omission of seeking the will of God affected Michal. She had settled in with a seemingly loving husband, but was ruthlessly ripped from her home as a non-entity pawn in a bargain between men. In addition, given the recent history between Abner, ruler of Saul's and then Ishbosheth's army, and Joab, head of David's army, where Abner killed Joab's brother, David should have discerned that there would be friction and war between the two. But David never sought the Lord. Later in the chapter, Joab killed Abner. In killing Abner, Joab himself, the formerly faithful servant of David who now felt betrayed that his lord had made a bargain with the enemy who killed his brother, showed non-submissive qualities. He went against David's desires, and acted treacherously. In addition, what he did as vengeance for his brother's blood was against the Mosaic Law (Numbers 35:22–28). To compound the damning effects of this flesh-led saga, David invoked horrible curses on Joab and his family for generations. This did not go well. We must always seek God first before venturing into things; failure to do so has deadly and far-reaching repercussions.

Prayer: Lord, please help me to seek you in every area of my life. Give me wisdom and divine direction. Direct my paths, oh Lord, let me be obedient to your Word and not lean on my own understanding. Help me to recognize how much I need you in every way, in Jesus' name. Amen.

Just Because He Ordains It Doesn't Mean It's Easy

2 Samuel 5:1–5

Then came all the tribes of Israel to David unto Hebron, and spake, saying, Behold, we are thy bone and thy flesh.

Also in time past, when Saul was king over us, thou wast he that leddest out and broughtest in Israel: and the LORD said to thee, Thou shalt feed my people Israel, and thou shalt be a captain over Israel.

So all the elders of Israel came to the king to Hebron; and king David made a league with them in Hebron before the LORD: and they anointed David king over Israel.

David was thirty years old when he began to reign, and he reigned forty years.

In Hebron he reigned over Judah seven years and six months: and in Jerusalem he reigned thirty and three years over all Israel and Judah.

(2 Samuel 5:1–5)

F inally, David was anointed king over all Israel and Judah. Finally, he was king over all of God's chosen people. This is a good time to reflect on all that David went through from the time he was ordained to be king to the time he actually reigned as king. It is easy to see David's mountaintop experience and ignore or overlook his years spent in the valley. This was David's third anointing—his first being when he was just a boy, now he was thirty years old.

As believers, we ought to understand that just because something is the divine will and plan of God for our lives does not mean it is going to be easy. Just because God has ordained certain things in and for our lives does not mean that it will be easy getting them, even when we follow His divine plan. From his boyhood, David had been chosen and ordained by God to be king over His people, yet it took him many years— almost two decades—immeasurable pain, heartache, and trials before He could assume His God-ordained position. David was despised, tricked, and hunted like a wild animal by the reigning king. He lived in caves and rocks, and had to beg for refuge. In all this time, David had the promise of what the end would look like, but the manifestation seemed nearly impossible at some points.

One thing was for sure, God had given David the grace to go through it all like a true champion. During that period of being in the proverbial valley, before he was exalted to the mountaintop, God led David through many things to build his integrity, establish His character, and intensify his relationship with, dependence on, and trust in God. He does have a divine plan, and He will get you there in His timing, but He will also lead you through certain experiences to mould and prepare you for what lies ahead. God will give us the grace that is necessary to weather the storm before the sun comes out. Rest assured that God has already promised that He will not allow us to be tempted above that which we can bear (1 Corinthians 10:13). He assures us in His Word that He is not a man that He should lie; what He has promised you, He will bring to pass (Numbers 23:19). So for the fulfillment of what He has promised you, *"Wait on the Lord, be of good courage, and He will strengthen your heart"* (Psalm 27:14).

Prayer: Oh Lord, I thank you for your promises to me, and for all the good things you have ordained for my life. Help me to not give up in the difficult seasons between the promise and its manifestation. Help me to trust in you with all my heart and to wait on you for the fulfillment of your Word, in Jesus' name. Amen.

A God of Standards

2 Samuel 6:1–7

Again, David gathered together all the chosen men of Israel, thirty thousand.

And David arose, and went with all the people that were with him from Baale of Judah, to bring up from thence the ark of God, whose name is called by the name of the LORD of hosts that dwelleth between the cherubims.

And they set the ark of God upon a new cart, and brought it out of the house of Abinadab that was in Gibeah: and Uzzah and Ahio, the sons of Abinadab, drave the new cart.

And they brought it out of the house of Abinadab which was at Gibeah, accompanying the ark of God: and Ahio went before the ark.

And David and all the house of Israel played before the LORD on all manner of instruments made of fir wood, even on harps, and on psalteries, and on timbrels, and on cornets, and on cymbals.

And when they came to Nachon's threshing floor, Uzzah put forth his hand to the ark of God, and took hold of it; for the oxen shook it.

And the anger of the LORD was kindled against Uzzah; and God smote him there for his error; and there he died by the ark of God.

(2 Samuel 6:1–7)

Our obedience to God is crucial to our living a full and blessed life. We must yield to the ways of God, despite our situations or the circumstances surrounding our decisions. The ark of God, according to Numbers 4:4–15, was to be carried on the shoulders of the priests, not on a cart, regardless of its opulence or newness. For whatever reason, perhaps convenience or efficiency, David thought it would be better to carry the ark on a cart, despite the specific standards set by God.

Many of us can find circumstances where we can justify our compromise, or disobedience, or partial obedience, or delayed obedience, to God. But in the sight of a holy God, it is never justifiable. Once our compromise is based on self, flesh, and human reasoning, it is never justifiable, and can cost us dearly. The Bible says that those who are willing and obedient will eat the good of the land, but they that backbite and rebel shall be devoured by the sword (Isaiah 1:19–20). We are also of the opinion that we can give God what we want, when and how we want, but that is incorrect; just reflect on the story of Cain and Abel (Genesis 4:1–15). God is a God of standards, and is never obligated to accept anything less than what He desires. Think of that when you gather for worship. Is it in spirit and in truth? Are you even involved? Are you giving according to what God has laid upon your heart and placed in His Word? One thing that saddens me is when believers act as though we are doing God a favour when we are in a time of praise, or when we are doing things for His glory. He is not begging. He deserves it! Give unto the Lord the glory due to His name (Psalm 29:2).

It is God's way or the highway. Such accounts ought to put the fear of God in our lives. We cannot do whatever we please, however we please, and expect God to accept it. We must do things God's way, according to His standards and outline.

Prayer: Father, in the name of Jesus, help me to be obedient to your Word, to crucify my flesh, and to let your standards be my will. I pray that the Spirit of God will lead me in times of uncertainty, and that as your sheep I will know your voice and heed it. Amen.

A Multifaceted God

2 Samuel 6:8–11

And David was displeased, because the LORD had made a breach upon Uzzah: and he called the name of the place Perezuzzah to this day.

And David was afraid of the LORD that day, and said, How shall the ark of the LORD come to me?

So David would not remove the ark of the LORD unto him into the city of David: but David carried it aside into the house of Obededom the Gittite.

And the ark of the LORD continued in the house of Obededom the Gittite three months: and the LORD blessed Obededom, and all his household.

(2 Samuel 6:8–11)

❈

One has to appreciate the complexity of God and, quite frankly, His sense of humour. God had just smitten a well-intentioned, albeit irreverent and disobedient, man for not doing things exactly as He had outlined. He killed Uzzah for touching the ark in an attempt to hold it up from falling. As a result of the breach, fear fell upon David, and he dumped the ark at someone's house. Unfazed, God continued to be faithful, just, and true to His promises. He blessed the household where the ark was left, tremendously, for all to see.

We often try to paint God as a single-story God, or as a one-dimensional being, but He is far from that. He is a God of wrath (Romans 1:18) and vengeance (Nahum 1:2), and the Bible says it is a fearful thing to fall into the hands of the living God (Hebrews 10:31). He is a God who hates sin, and deals with it harshly; after all, there is a hell. But the Bible also tells us that His anger endures but for a moment, and in His favour is life (Psalm 30:5). He is also a God of tremendous grace and mercy (Psalm 103:8–13, 17). He is a God of unconditional love (Romans 8:35–39), whose mercies are new every morning (Lamentations 3:22–23) and whose blessings make rich and add no sorrow (Proverbs 10:22).

The amazing thing about God is that He is very clear about what aspects of our behaviour evoke His various qualities (Isaiah 1:19–20). He does not leave it up to chance, or just surprise us. Our duty is to study the Word of God to avoid being ignorant of His ways, as Uzzah probably was. We know in our obedience to Him that His precepts are peace, joy, and everlasting life. Conversely, we know that a life of disobedience will only lead to condemnation and everlasting damnation. He is not a one-dimensional God. He is multifaceted, but He doesn't change (Malachi 3:6; Hebrews 13:8). He makes it plain for us to understand His ways, since His nature is love, and He wants to bless us.

Prayer: Father, I thank you for truth and clarity that comes from your Word. I thank you for the Holy Spirit who sensitizes me when I displease you. And I thank you for grace. Help me to diligently study your Word and hide it in my heart that I may not sin against you. Amen.

Joy in the Presence
of the Lord

2 Samuel 6:12–19

And it was told king David, saying, The LORD hath blessed the house of Obededom, and all that pertaineth unto him, because of the ark of God. So David went and brought up the ark of God from the house of Obededom into the city of David with gladness.

And it was so, that when they that bare the ark of the LORD had gone six paces, he sacrificed oxen and fatlings. And David danced before the LORD with all his might; and David was girded with a linen ephod.

So David and all the house of Israel brought up the ark of the LORD with shouting, and with the sound of the trumpet. And as the ark of the LORD came into the city of David, Michal Saul's daughter looked through a window, and saw King David leaping and dancing before the LORD; and she despised him in her heart.

And they brought in the ark of the LORD, and set it in his place, in the midst of the tabernacle that David had pitched for it: and David offered burnt offerings and peace offerings before the LORD. And as soon as David had made an end of offering burnt offerings and peace offerings, he blessed the people in the name of the LORD *of hosts. And he dealt among all the people, even among the whole multitude of Israel, as well to the women as men, to every one a cake of bread, and a good piece of flesh, and a flagon of wine. So all the people departed every one to his house.*

(2 Samuel 6:12–19)

⎯⎯◆◆◆⎯⎯

There is no way you can be surrounded by the glory of God and not be overwhelmed with awe and pleasant emotions. Joy, peace, contentment, and exuberance fill the hearts and souls of those who are in the presence of God and are seeking Him. For in the presence of God there is fullness of joy, and at His right hand are pleasures forevermore (Psalm 16:11).

David was ecstatic that He could finally bring the ark of the Lord, which represented His presence, into his city. He was beside himself with ecstasy, dancing with all his might. He paid no attention to his title or position; all he wanted to do was worship God and give Him all the glory due to Him.

Unfortunately, some people can be in the presence of God and not experience this supernatural joy. Like Michal, many engage in religious activities, like going to church, without really seeking the fullness of God or an encounter with God. Instead, they go with a host of motives other than glorifying God, seemingly unimpressed that they are in the presence of a holy, righteous, loving, and awesome God. The Word of

God in Jeremiah 29:13 says that when you seek God with your heart, you will find Him. Sadly, some people go to church but won't even sing the songs or engage in the service in any way. Others merely recite things as ritual, with no heart or soul connection, and then wonder why they leave so dry, empty, and unedified.

A wise woman at my church always says, "What you put into the service is what you will get out of it." Another one says, "Don't be a spectator in the house of God, be an active participant." When we enter the presence of God, we ought to lose ourselves and allow Him to take control. Anyone who knows who God is, and what He has done and continues to do, will worship Him. Don't let your mind become filled with other things. Focus on God, and finding joy in His presence will be as natural as breathing. Give unto God the glory that He deserves, and what comes back to us will be most fulfilling and transformative.

Prayer: Father in Heaven, please help me to find joy in your presence. Let my mind not wander or stray from your awesomeness. Let my thoughts be filled with the wonder of who you are and all that you have done for me. Give me grace to seek you with all my heart, so that I may find you, in Jesus' name. Amen.

The Cost of Praise

2 Samuel 6:16, 20–23

And as the ark of the LORD came into the city of David, Michal Saul's daughter looked through a window, and saw king David leaping and dancing before the LORD; and she despised him in her heart.

Then David returned to bless his household. And Michal the daughter of Saul came out to meet David, and said, How glorious was the king of Israel to day, who uncovered himself to day in the eyes of the handmaids of his servants, as one of the vain fellows shamelessly uncovereth himself!

And David said unto Michal, It was before the LORD, which chose me before thy father, and before all his house, to appoint me ruler over the people of the LORD, over Israel: therefore will I play before the LORD. And I will yet be more vile than thus, and will be base in mine own sight: and of the maidservants which thou hast spoken of, of them shall I be had in honour.

Therefore Michal the daughter of Saul had no child unto the day of her death.

(2 Samuel 6:16, 20–23)

One cannot help but develop a soft spot for Michal. She had been victimized many times over by the men in her life and was worthy of some form of justification. But when God is in something, there is no excuse to go against it. Michal's criticism of David stemmed from the fact that she didn't fully understand the cost of his praise. When we see people in church, and elsewhere, glorifying God with all that they have, or "making a fool of themselves" in our eyes, we must recognize that we don't know what they've been through, or where God has brought them from, or what it takes for them to worship Him with such zeal and enthusiasm. Did Michal have any idea what God had done for David? Did she have any idea that had it not been for God David would have either been dead or still tending sheep? Did she know that God had chosen him to be king over all his brothers, when not even his father believed in him? Did she know that God had saved him from death by lions and bears and a giant? Did she know that God had kept him when her father had relentlessly hunted him to destroy him? Did she know that God had given him uncommon favour with his enemies while He was preparing him to take the throne? How could she use a role that God himself had called and anointed David for as the reason he should withhold his praises? God had made David king. How then could that role be the reason He could not worship God with abandon? Michal had no clue who God was to David, and so she couldn't possibly understand the cost of his worship.

Too often, we put stipulations on what acceptable worship looks like, and we turn our noses up at those who don't do it our way. Even worse, we often say that it's not of God or it's fleshly, while having no insight into the person's heart. We even condemn types of music and the ministers that sing them. Many people tend to think that Gospel or Christian music should sound a certain way or have a certain tempo, and completely disregard certain genres of music because they don't suit their taste, so they assume they cannot suit God's either. But what do you do with someone who has been singing reggae, soca, rap, or rock in the world, or who simply has a passion for a specific genre, and who is obviously very gifted at what they do? Surely, gifts come from God, and He didn't save these individuals to mute them. God's requirement for worship is that it is done in spirit and in truth (John 4:24), and He judges our hearts. How is it that the church—yes, you and I—judges based on personal preferences? Let us seek discernment, because if God is in it, there is no justification to go against it.

Prayer: Father, in the name of Jesus, please forgive me for the times I have judged and condemned others' service wrongfully. Please give me the spirit of discernment that I may see through your eyes. Help me to worship you in spirit and in truth, and not be bound by my desire to please others or conform to manmade standards. I thank you for who you are and all that you have done. You deserve my worship. Amen.

Never Ungrateful

2 Samuel 9 & 19:31–40

And David said, Is there yet any that is left of the house of Saul, that I may shew him kindness for Jonathan's sake? And there was of the house of Saul a servant whose name was Ziba. And when they had called him unto David, the king said unto him, Art thou Ziba? And he said, Thy servant is he. And the king said, Is there not yet any of the house of Saul, that I may shew the kindness of God unto him? And Ziba said unto the king, Jonathan hath yet a son, which is lame on his feet. And the king said unto him, Where is he? And Ziba said unto the king, Behold, he is in the house of Machir, the son of Ammiel, in Lodebar. Then king David sent, and fetched him out of the house of Machir, the son of Ammiel, from Lodebar.

Now when Mephibosheth, the son of Jonathan, the son of Saul, was come unto David, he fell on his face, and did reverence. And David said, Mephibosheth. And he answered, Behold thy servant! And David said unto him, Fear not: for I will surely shew thee kindness for Jonathan thy father's sake, and will restore thee all the land of Saul thy father; and thou shalt eat bread at my table continually. And he bowed himself, and said, What is thy servant, that thou shouldest look upon such a dead dog as I am? Then the king called to Ziba, Saul's servant, and said unto him, I have given unto thy master's son all that pertained to Saul and to all his house. Thou therefore, and thy sons, and thy servants, shall till the land for him, and thou shalt bring in the fruits, that thy master's son may have food to eat: but Mephibosheth thy master's son shall eat bread always at my table. Now Ziba had fifteen sons and twenty servants. Then said Ziba unto the king, According to all that my lord the king hath commanded his servant, so shall thy servant do. As for Mephibosheth, said the king, he shall eat at my table, as one of the king's sons. And Mephibosheth had a young son, whose name was Micha. And all that dwelt in the house of Ziba were servants unto Mephibosheth. So Mephibosheth dwelt in Jerusalem: for he did eat continually at the king's table; and was lame on both his feet.

(2 Samuel 9)

And Barzillai the Gileadite came down from Rogelim, and went over Jordan with the king, to conduct him over Jordan. Now Barzillai was a very aged man, even fourscore years old: and he had provided the king of sustenance while he lay at Mahanaim; for he was a very great man. And the king said unto Barzillai, Come thou over with me, and I will feed thee with me in Jerusalem. And Barzillai said unto the king, How long have I to live, that I should go up with the king unto Jerusalem? I am this day fourscore years old: and can I discern between good and evil? can thy servant taste what I eat or what I drink? can I hear any more the voice of singing men and singing women? wherefore then should thy servant be yet a burden unto my lord the king? Thy servant will go a little way over Jordan with the king: and why should the king recompense it me with such a reward? Let thy servant, I pray thee, turn back again, that I may die in mine own city, and be buried by the grave of my father and of my mother. But behold thy servant Chimham; let him go over with my lord the king; and do to him what shall seem good unto thee. And the king answered, Chimham shall go over with me, and I will do to him that which shall seem good unto thee: and whatsoever thou shalt require of me, that will I do for thee. And all the people went over Jordan. And when the king was come over, the king kissed Barzillai, and blessed him; and he returned unto his own place. Then the king went on to Gilgal, and Chimham went on with him: and all the people of Judah conducted the king, and also half the people of Israel.

(2 Samuel 19:31-40)

———◈◈◈———

David never forgot an act of kindness. He made note of those who helped him or somehow or another enabled him to be in a position of blessing, influence, and power. In the case of Mephibosheth, David actively sought out someone related to Jonathan whom he could show kindness to honour the covenant made between him and Jonathan (1 Samuel 20). David deemed the bond shared between him and Saul's son, and the extent to which Jonathan went to shield David from his father, as not easily dismissed, though Jonathan was now dead. He looked for someone else to bless. He sought to honour what Jonathan had done by passing on the blessing. The case of Barzillai, in 2 Samuel 19, reveals that same spirit of honour in David. For the kindness that Barzillai had shown to him when he was in exile, the king now sought to repay him with kindness. And even when Barzillai refused it for himself, David acquiesced to pass it on to Barzillai's servant.

It is important for us not to be ungrateful or forgetful of those who have been kind to us. Ungratefulness and forgetfulness can be toxic. We must always recognize those who have sacrificed, or were blessings out of their abundance, in order to enable us to attain both in the spiritual and in the natural. None of us have gotten to where we are by ourselves. Others have paved the way or mentored us or supported us in one way or another. Be a blessing. It's not that we are to only do good to those that do good to us, but recognizing and repaying someone's kindness is important, even when that means passing it on to others related, or unrelated, to the source of the blessing. When we get to a place of achievement, we are to do for others what those before us did for us. Don't be ungrateful. Let people know they've been a blessing, and become one yourself.

Prayer: Father, I thank you for all of your blessings towards me. Thank you for the people you have placed in my life or have sent before me to pave the way. For family, mentors, friends, and those who have influenced my achievements, I thank you. Help me to be a blessing, to do for those who have blessed me, and for others, whatever is within my power, so that they, too, can achieve. Help me to be vigilant for opportunities to bless others, in Jesus' name. Amen.

Falling Prey to Sin

2 Samuel 11

And it came to pass, after the year was expired, at the time when kings go forth to battle, that David sent Joab, and his servants with him, and all Israel; and they destroyed the children of Ammon, and besieged Rabbah. But David tarried still at Jerusalem.

And it came to pass in an eveningtide, that David arose from off his bed, and walked upon the roof of the king's house: and from the roof he saw a woman washing herself; and the woman was very beautiful to look upon. And David sent and enquired after the woman. And one said, Is not this Bathsheba, the daughter of Eliam, the wife of Uriah the Hittite? And David sent messengers, and took her; and she came in unto him, and he lay with her; for she was purified from her uncleanness: and she returned unto her house. And the woman conceived, and sent and told David, and said, I am with child.

And David sent to Joab, saying, Send me Uriah the Hittite. And Joab sent Uriah to David. And when Uriah was come unto him, David demanded of him how Joab did, and how the people did, and how the war prospered.

And David said to Uriah, Go down to thy house, and wash thy feet. And Uriah departed out of the king's house, and there followed him a mess of meat from the king. But Uriah slept at the door of the king's house with all the servants of his lord, and went not down to his house. And when they had told David, saying, Uriah went not down unto his house, David said unto Uriah, Camest thou not from thy journey? why then didst thou not go down unto thine house?

And Uriah said unto David, The ark, and Israel, and Judah, abide in tents; and my lord Joab, and the servants of my lord, are encamped in the open fields; shall I then go into mine house, to eat and to drink, and to lie with my wife? as thou livest, and as thy soul liveth, I will not do this thing.

And David said to Uriah, Tarry here today also, and tomorrow I will let thee depart. So Uriah abode in Jerusalem that day, and the morrow.

[1]*And when David had called him, he did eat and drink before him; and he made him drunk: and at even he went out to lie on his bed with the servants of his lord, but went not down to his house. And it came to pass in the morning, that David wrote a letter to Joab, and sent it by the hand of Uriah. And he wrote in the letter, saying, Set ye Uriah in the forefront of the hottest battle, and retire ye from him, that he may be smitten, and die.*

And it came to pass, when Joab observed the city, that he assigned Uriah unto a place where he knew that valiant men were. And the men of the city went out, and fought with Joab: and there fell some of the people of the servants of David; and Uriah the Hittite died also. Then Joab sent and told David all the things concerning the war; and charged the messenger, saying, When thou hast made an end of telling the matters of the war unto the king, and if so be that the king's wrath arise, and he say unto thee, Wherefore approached ye so nigh unto the city when ye did fight? knew ye not that they would shoot from the wall? Who smote Abimelech the son of Jerubbesheth? did not a woman cast a piece of a millstone upon him from the wall, that he died in Thebez? why went ye nigh the wall? then say thou, Thy servant Uriah the Hittite is dead also.

So the messenger went, and came and shewed David all that Joab had sent him for. And the messenger said unto David, Surely the men prevailed against us, and came out unto us into the field, and we were upon them even unto the entering of the gate. And the shooters shot from off the wall upon thy servants; and some of the king's servants be dead, and thy servant Uriah the Hittite is dead also.

Then David said unto the messenger, Thus shalt thou say unto Joab, Let not this thing displease thee, for the sword devoureth one as well as another: make thy battle more strong against the city, and overthrow it: and encourage thou him.

And when the wife of Uriah heard that Uriah her husband was dead, she mourned for her husband. And when the mourning was past, David sent and fetched her to his house, and she became his wife, and bare him a son. But the thing that David had done displeased the LORD.

(2 Samuel 11)

———❊———

It's amazing how the best of us fall prey to the plan of the enemy and fail God sometimes. David was indeed a man after God's own heart, and no one could doubt his love for God. But it is often said that the devil finds work for idle hands to do. And so David sinned against God in the most atrocious of ways—adultery and murder. Had David been where he was supposed to be, off at war like all the other kings, then he would not have seen Bathsheba bathing on her rooftop. Sometimes, after or during spiritual peaks in our lives, we tend to get high-minded, proud, and arrogant. But the Bible says that anyone who thinks that he or she stands should take heed lest they fall (1 Corinthians 10:12). We are to always walk humbly before the Lord, relying heavily on the Holy Spirit to lead us into the paths of righteousness. We are to be very wary of self-righteousness and callousness to sin. And as Jesus said to His disciples, we are to watch and pray lest we fall into temptation, for the spirit is willing, but the flesh is weak (Matthew 24:41). Another thing that makes us susceptible to sin is our loss of perspective; we forget that we are to do all things as unto God (1 Corinthians 10:31). So we get disheartened and discouraged sometimes, because we may feel underappreciated. Or sometimes we just get tired of doing the right things all the time, and feel like doing the not-so-right thing just once won't hurt. But again the Bible reminds us to *"not be weary in well doing: for in due season we shall reap, if we faint not"* (Galatians 6:9).

Watch and beware of your own weaknesses, the things that make you vulnerable to temptation. As the Word says, we are drawn away according to our own lusts (James 1:14). The enemy does not tempt us with things that we are not interested in; he knows our weaknesses. We, too, should know our individual weaknesses and walk alert every day, mortifying the flesh lest we fall into heinous sins. We are to watch, be alert and vigilant, for the things that hinder us from doing what we are supposed to do. Every decision has a consequence; whether we choose to commit or omit, there are repercussions for our decisions. Therefore, we must choose wisely, and ask God for grace and wisdom and strength to keep doing the right things in every season of our lives.

Prayer: Father in Heaven, please lead me in paths of righteousness, for your name's sake. Help me to walk in the spirit, so that I may not fulfill the lusts of the flesh. In my areas of weakness, empower me with your divine strength. May I so fully desire your righteousness and your will that there is no space for lusting after the things of this world or giving in to sinful flesh, in Jesus' name. Amen.

Overcoming Sin

2 Samuel 12:5–27

And David's anger was greatly kindled against the man; and he said to Nathan, As the LORD liveth, the man that hath done this thing shall surely die: and he shall restore the lamb fourfold, because he did this thing, and because he had no pity. And Nathan said to David, Thou art the man. Thus saith the LORD God of Israel, I anointed thee king over Israel, and I delivered thee out of the hand of Saul; and I gave thee thy master's house, and thy master's wives into thy bosom, and gave thee the house of Israel and of Judah; and if that had been too little, I would moreover have given unto thee such and such things. Wherefore hast thou despised the commandment of the LORD, to do evil in his sight? thou hast killed Uriah the Hittite with the sword, and hast taken his wife to be thy wife, and hast slain him with the sword of the children of Ammon. Now therefore the sword shall never depart from thine house; because thou hast despised me, and hast taken the wife of Uriah the Hittite to be thy wife. Thus saith the LORD, Behold, I will raise up evil against thee out of thine own house, and I will take thy wives before thine eyes, and give them unto thy neighbour, and he shall lie with thy wives in the sight of this sun. For thou didst it secretly: but I will do this thing before all Israel, and before the sun. And David said unto Nathan, I have sinned against the LORD. And Nathan said unto David, The LORD also hath put away thy sin; thou shalt not die. Howbeit, because by this deed thou hast given great occasion to the enemies of the LORD to blaspheme, the child also that is born unto thee shall surely die. And Nathan departed unto his house. And the LORD struck the child that Uriah's wife bare unto David, and it was very sick. David therefore besought God for the child; and David fasted, and went in, and lay all night upon the earth. And the elders of his house arose, and went to him, to raise him up from the earth: but he would not, neither did he eat bread with them. And it came to pass on the seventh day, that the child died. And the servants of David feared to tell him that the child was dead: for they said, Behold, while the child was yet alive, we spake unto him, and he would not hearken unto our voice: how will he then vex himself, if we tell him that the child is dead? But when David saw that his servants whispered, David perceived that the child was dead: therefore David said unto his servants, Is the child dead? And they said, He is dead. Then David arose from the earth, and washed, and anointed himself, and changed his apparel, and came into the house of the LORD, and worshipped: then he came to his own house; and when he required, they set bread before him, and he did eat. Then said his servants unto him, What thing is this that thou hast done? thou didst fast and weep for the child, while it was alive; but when the child was dead, thou didst rise and eat bread. And he said, While the child was yet alive, I fasted and wept: for I said, Who can tell whether GOD will be gracious to me, that the child may live? But now he is dead, wherefore should I fast? can I bring him back again? I shall go to him, but he shall not return to me.

And David comforted Bathsheba his wife, and went in unto

her, and lay with her: and she bare a son, and he called his name Solomon: and the LORD loved him. And he sent by the hand of Nathan the prophet; and he called his name Jedidiah, because of the LORD.

And Joab fought against Rabbah of the children of Ammon, and took the royal city. And Joab sent messengers to David, and said, I have fought against Rabbah, and have taken the city of waters.

(2 Samuel 12:5–27)

—⊶⊰⊱⊷—

Whenever we sin, we have a choice to either hatch a cover-up, simple or elaborate, or repent. Clearly, anything outside of repentance and the will of God is of the devil. He often deceives us by making us believe that we will be okay, as long as no one finds out. What we don't realize, until it's too late, is that covering up one sin often leads to the commission of others. Not all of us kill someone else to cover up our sin, for some of us it's telling lies. We get lured into the false belief that our sins will not be found out, when the Bible clearly tells us that whatever is hidden will come to light (Luke 18:17). The enemy himself will taunt and torment us with the sin, heaping condemnation and guilt upon us. We cannot get away with sin. God will eventually expose sin, not to bring us to condemnation, but to bring us to repentance, so we won't continue to wallow in sin and be deceived, thinking that no one sees, no one knows, or no one cares.

We all sin and fall short of the glory of God (Romans 3:23).

God knew we would sin before we sinned; nevertheless, He requires us to be holy, because He is holy (Leviticus 11:44). Hence, He has given us an advocate in Christ Jesus (1 John 2:1). We must repent and turn from sin by the grace of God. Sometimes we tell ourselves that our deceits or cover-ups are to protect those around us from getting hurt or from causing irreversible repercussions. The truth is, sin has consequences, every action does. However, we never know for sure what the consequences may be when we repent. Sometimes, even when we repent, we do not escape earthly penalties or ramifications (vv. 7–12). But a genuine heart simply wants to be in right standing with God, and that is what repentance offers. David himself wrote, in response to this sin, that a broken and contrite heart God will not despise (Psalm 51:17). Even when we don't deserve it, God is a God of mercy.

If you are struggling with concealed sin, then pray about it. Genuinely repent before God and ask Him for the wisdom and grace to forsake the sin and break free from the stronghold. Also, ask Him for the right time, person or people to come clean to, and ask Him to work it out. There are no promises or guarantees on how things will work out, but we are obeying the Word when we confess our faults and sins to one another (James 5:16). In doing so, we are also breaking the power of the enemy over us, making ourselves accountable to others, and gaining a partner in prayer to overcome the sin. It is very liberating when the enemy can't hold anything over your head and cause you to live in fear that one day he might reveal it.

Prayer: Father, I confess my sins to you. I admit that I have done wrong and have fallen short of your glory. Please forgive me. Give me grace, dear God, to do that which is right in your sight. Break the power of sin over my life, and help me to live a life that pleases you, in Jesus' name. Amen.

Never Beyond the Grace of God

2 Samuel 12:1–6, 13

And the Lord sent Nathan unto David. And he came unto him, and said unto him, There were two men in one city; the one rich, and the other poor.

*The rich man had exceeding many flocks and herds: but the poor man had nothing, save one little ewe lamb, which he had bough*t and nourished up: and it grew up together with him, and with his children; it did eat of his own meat, and drank of his own cup, and lay in his bosom, and was unto him as a daughter.

And there came a traveller unto the rich man, and he spared to take of his own flock and of his own herd, to dress for the wayfaring man that was come unto him; but took the poor man's lamb, and dressed it for the man that was come to him.

And David's anger was greatly kindled against the man; and he said to Nathan, As the Lord liveth, the man that hath done this thing shall surely die:

And he shall restore the lamb fourfold, because he did this thing, and because he had no pity. And Nathan said to David, Thou art the man.

And David said unto Nathan, I have sinned against the LORD. And Nathan said unto David, The LORD also hath put away thy sin; thou shalt not die.

(2 Samuel 12:1–7a, 13)

———⬥⬥⬥———

It's amazing how our self-righteousness is only operable when it pertains to someone else's unrighteousness. David's response to Nathan's story reminds us of Jesus' rebuke in Matthew 7:1–5. We are being very hypocritical when we see and try to remove the speck of sawdust in our brethren's eye yet ignore the plank of wood in our own. How often do we overlook our own sins and, like David, seek to apply the full measure of the law and judgement—that we so conveniently remember—on people who have committed lesser or equivalent sins. Too often we apply grace, compassion, and understanding to ourselves, while we judge and condemn others. We require grace from God but administer quick and harsh judgements on others. This is a prime example of when our "righteous indignation" is merely pseudo-righteousness. Let us not be too eager to discard our foundational doctrines of forgiveness and love. Instead, let those who are spiritual restore those who have fallen, in the spirit of meekness (Galatians 6:1).

For those who have fallen, remember that you are never beyond the grace of God. Regardless of where you've been or what you've done, God's mercies are new every morning (Lamentations 3:22–23). His mercy is from everlasting to everlasting, and you don't have to deserve it. We all have sinned and fallen short of the glory of God, but the real tragedy is when we wallow in sin. One of the reasons we often stay in sin is that we are deceived by the father of lies (John 8:44). He fills our heads with lies, like "Why bother trying, when you know you'll never get it right?" or "You will never be able to fully overcome this sin," or "You've gone too far for the grace of God." He tries to condemn us and weary our spirits so we cannot repent and throw ourselves at the mercy of God. But God wants you to come back home. Forgiveness is only a prayer away. True repentance acknowledges sin, is genuinely sorry for the commission of sin, and earnestly seeks to be free from that sin. And, amazingly, not only will God forgive your sins if you ask, but He will also give you the grace to overcome your strongholds and areas of weakness. That such abominations in the life of David could lead to such an eloquent and earnest prayer in Psalm 51, which many believers use today in their prayers for repentance, is a testament to the grace of God.

Prayer: Father, in the name of Jesus, forgive me of my sins and restore me to right standing with you. Empty me of my desire to engage in sinful activity, so that all my ways may please you. Thank you for grace, mercy, and restoration. Guide me by your love, and help me to apply mercy liberally to others when they fall short of your glory. Amen.

Sin and Disrepute

2 Samuel 12:14

Howbeit, because by this deed thou hast given great occasion to the enemies of the LORD to blaspheme, the child also that is born unto thee shall surely die.

(2 Samuel 12:14)

———— ❖❖❖ ————

One of the worst results of sin in a believer's life is the disrepute it brings to God and the faith. The prophet Nathan brings up the fact that David's sinful deeds have given the enemies of the Lord a reason to blaspheme, and because of that, the baby conceived in his sin would die.

The reasons why the enemy will never cover up our sins for long is that firstly, he can use it to cause other believers to fall away from the faith or become weakened in the faith, and secondly, he can also use it to make unbelievers disregard the gospel, the church, our God, and our witness.

Many people use the sins and the faults of Christians as an excuse for not coming to Christ or not even visiting church. Hence, the enemy will incessantly tempt the people of God, then strategically expose their sinful deeds and bring them to open shame. This is all the more reason why we need to walk circumspectly, why we need to ask God for strength and grace and sustenance. None of us are beyond temptation. The Bible tells us that the enemy goes about like a roaring lion, seeking whom he may devour (1 Peter 5:8). Our daily prayers need to include asking God to "lead us not into temptation," "deliver us from evil" (Matthew 6:13), and keep our feet from falling (Psalm 56:13). We need to daily ask God for grace to walk in the spirit (Galatians 5:16) and to put to death the deeds of the flesh (Romans 8:13; Colossians 3:5). God forbid we should become stumbling blocks or cause offense to others. May we never cause maturing believers to fall away from the faith, or unbelievers to refuse to come to God. Our witness matters, but sin and compromise mar that. We cannot allow the enemy to use us for his advantage.

Prayer: Father, in Jesus' name, help me to stand in the face of temptation. Help me to walk in the spirit so I may not give in to the desires of the flesh and bring disrepute to your name. Forgive me for every time I have unwittingly caused others to doubt you, diminish their faith, or speak badly against the church. I pray that their hearts will be healed and their faith restored. Give me grace to be an exemplary witness, for your name's sake. Amen.

Resting in the Divine Will of God

2 Samuel 12:16–23

David therefore besought God for the child; and David fasted, and went in, and lay all night upon the earth. And the elders of his house arose, and went to him, to raise him up from the earth: but he would not, neither did he eat bread with them.

And it came to pass on the seventh day, that the child died. And the servants of David feared to tell him that the child was dead: for they said, Behold, while the child was yet alive, we spake unto him, and he would not hearken unto our voice: how will he then vex himself, if we tell him that the child is dead?

But when David saw that his servants whispered, David perceived that the child was dead: therefore David said unto his servants, Is the child dead? And they said, He is dead. Then David arose from the earth, and washed, and anointed himself, and changed his apparel, and came into the house of the LORD, and worshipped: then he came to his own house; and when he required, they set bread before him, and he did eat.

Then said his servants unto him, What thing is this that thou hast done? thou didst fast and weep for the child, while it was alive; but when the child was dead, thou didst rise and eat bread.

And he said, While the child was yet alive, I fasted and wept: for I said, Who can tell whether GOD will be gracious to me, that the child may live? But now he is dead, wherefore should I fast? can I bring him back again? I shall go to him, but he shall not return to me.

(2 Samuel 12:16–23)

D avid's response to his gut-wrenching situation was so profound. Here was a man whose child was sick to the point of death after God pronounced judgement on him. At no point in his ordeal does the man of God wallow in self-pity or rebel against, or curse, God. David's response to this horrible situation shows his reliance on, and confidence in, God. Our mentor prayed and fasted fervently when the full extent of the situation became apparent. He fully trusted the power of prayer and the power of God to change things, if He so desired.

Hezekiah, too, was a man of God who believed in the power of fervent, effectual prayer to transform his situation, and was rewarded with fifteen additional years after the pronouncement of his death (2 Kings 20:1–6). Similarly, David threw himself on the mercy of God. He never rebelled against, or railed at, or cursed God. Job, too, refused to curse God when things became unbearable (Job 2:9–10). Instead, Job humbled himself and accepted whatsoever God allowed. David never asked why, proving that, like Job, he rested in the sovereign will of God. He showed confidence in the wisdom of God, that

He knew best and that He was in control. David also never wallowed in self-pity after the child died; he let it go. He got up, showered, anointed himself, ate, and was at peace. He only cried out to God when there was a chance that the situation could be changed. Once it was clear that God had shut the door, he was at peace. God had had the final say, and David rested in the divine will of God. He understood and accepted the power of God to open and close doors, according to His omniscience (Revelation 3:8a). Even when God's decision was not David's desire, he humbled himself, rested in the will of God, and was at peace.

What does our response to the hard situations in our life depict? Do we rebel against, or rail at, God? Do we ask why us and tell Him why we don't deserve the trials? Do we take matters into our own hands and try to fix the problem by human strength and genius? Do we wallow in self-pity, feeling sorry for ourselves, crying tears of defeat, sighing like no one knows or cares? Trust in the sovereign power of God. Believe that the steps of a good person are indeed ordered by God (Psalm 37:23). Believe that He will withhold nothing good from them that walk uprightly (Psalm 84:11). When God closes a door in your life, rest assured that it is for your good, and that He has a purpose for it.

Prayer: Father in Heaven, I trust you. I trust your divine will for my life. Even when I don't understand, or it feels incredibly difficult, I know that you know best, and you always keep my best interest at heart. Thank you for being omniscient, in Jesus' name. Amen.

Redeeming Love

2 Samuel 12:24–25

And David comforted Bathsheba his wife, and went in unto her, and lay with her: and she bare a son, and he called his name Solomon: and the Lord loved him.

And he sent by the hand of Nathan the prophet; and he called his name Jedidiah, because of the Lord.

(2 Samuel 12:24–25)

⊰⊹⊱

I t is so amazing that the Holy Spirit found it necessary to highlight the love of God for Solomon in such a profound way. Not only did the Spirit record that God loved Solomon, but God also sent His own prophet to name the baby "Jedidiah," which means "Beloved of the Lord." The grace of God is absolutely incredible.

That a boy born out of such a salaciously sinful situation should be declared and named by God to be His beloved provides several lessons. One is about the grace of God that the church must exhibit. We cannot condemn and cast out folks based on their backgrounds. Frankly, even if folks are currently struggling with sin, and desperately battling between good and evil, spirit and flesh, instead of condemning them, we must pray. Regardless of how sordid an individual's past is, God loves him or her with a redeeming love, and so should we, if we have the heart and mind of Christ. We, as believers, must always bear in mind that love covers a multitude of sins (1 Peter 4:8), and it is our duty to restore those that have fallen into sin (Galatians 6:1).

Another lesson is that genuine repentance is a powerful thing. Genuine repentance has the power to break strongholds, destroy curses, and set prisoners of sin free. Had David ignored or justified his sin, Solomon would probably not have been born, would surely not have been named "Beloved by the Lord," and certainly would not have been the chosen one, out of all the sons of David, to build the temple of God, rule Israel, and continue the Davidic legacy. So if you're struggling with sin or strongholds, genuinely repent and cry out to God from the depths of your soul. He will deliver you and make all things new.

Prayer: Lord, I thank you for redeeming love. I thank you that you respond to the repentant prayer from a broken and contrite heart, and cover sins with love. Help me to exhibit that same kind of love to others, so that people may acknowledge their sins before you and accept their fresh start, in Jesus' name. Amen.

There Is Wisdom in Reproof

2 Samuel 13:1–5

And it came to pass after this, that Absalom the son of David had a fair sister, whose name was Tamar; and Amnon the son of David loved her.

And Amnon was so vexed, that he fell sick for his sister Tamar; for she was a virgin; and Amnon thought it hard for him to do anything to her.

But Amnon had a friend, whose name was Jonadab, the son of Shimeah David's brother: and Jonadab was a very subtil man.

And he said unto him, Why art thou, being the king's son, lean from day to day? Wilt thou not tell me? And Amnon said unto him, I love Tamar, my brother Absalom's sister.

And Jonadab said unto him, Lay thee down on thy bed, and make thyself sick: and when thy father cometh to see thee, say unto him, I pray thee, let my sister Tamar come, and give me meat, and dress the meat in my sight, that I may see it, and eat it at her hand.

(2 Samuel 13:1–5)

Words of wisdom, or an on-time reproof from the right source, are crucial for the prevention of countless catastrophes. Had Jonadab rebuked his friend's sinful desires, he would have saved Amnon's life. Even more glaring is the fact that there is no record of David, father of both the survivor and the perpetrator of this atrocious crime, reproving Amnon for his sin. The Bible records that David was "wroth," but there is no record of any consequences that he enforced. Had David taken steps to correct the situation as it required, Absalom would not have felt the urge to avenge his sister's rape. David might have loved his children to a fault and might have, albeit subconsciously, neglected to reprove Amnon because of this misguided love. However, Proverbs 13:24 reminds us that those who fail to discipline their children actually hate them.

We are to be wise about who we take counsel from, what counsel we give, and what we withhold. Not all advice from seemingly well-intentioned people is good for us. Beware of people who will always tell you what you want to hear and never challenge, correct, or rebuke you. Likewise, beware of always telling others what they want to hear and never challenging, correcting, or rebuking in love and wisdom.

We also have to make it conducive for others to give us constructive criticism and tell us the truth. Some people use different means, whether consciously, overtly, or covertly, to get people to never oppose them. Some of those means include fear, hostility, and emotional manipulation. If others withhold wise counsel and reproof for fear of upsetting or offending you, it will be detrimental to your growth in every area of life. Only scoffers hate others when they are reproved, the wise receive instruction and increase in wisdom as a result (Proverbs 9:8–9). Therefore, seek wisdom in giving counsel, and humility in receiving it. It has the power to avert many ills.

Prayer: Father in Heaven, I thank you for the Holy Spirit, who gives wise counsel and convicts me of my wrong. I pray that you will fill my heart with humility, love, and wisdom, so that I may give and receive reproof that lines up with your Word and standards, in Jesus' name. Amen.

Following Divine Direction

2 Samuel 14 & 18

Now Joab the son of Zeruiah perceived that the king's heart was toward Absalom. And Joab sent to Tekoah, and fetched thence a wise woman, and said unto her, I pray thee, feign thyself to be a mourner, and put on now mourning apparel, and anoint not thyself with oil, but be as a woman that had a long time mourned for the dead: and come to the king, and speak on this manner unto him. So Joab put the words in her mouth. And when the woman of Tekoah spake to the king, she fell on her face to the ground, and did obeisance, and said, Help, O king.

And the king said unto her, What aileth thee? And she answered, I am indeed a widow woman, and mine husband is dead. And thy handmaid had two sons, and they two strove together in the field, and there was none to part them, but the one smote the other, and slew him. And, behold, the whole family is risen against thine handmaid, and they said, Deliver him that smote his brother, that we may kill him, for the life of his brother whom he slew; and we will destroy the heir also: and so they shall quench my coal which is left, and shall not leave to my husband neither name nor remainder upon the earth. And the king said unto the woman, Go to thine house, and I will give charge concerning thee.

And the woman of Tekoah said unto the king, My lord, O king, the iniquity be on me, and on my father's house: and the king and his throne be guiltless. And the king said, Whoever saith ought unto thee, bring him to me, and he shall not touch thee any more. Then said she, I pray thee, let the king remember the LORD thy God, that thou wouldest not suffer the revengers of blood to destroy any more, lest they destroy my son. And he said, As the LORD liveth, there shall not one hair of thy son fall to the earth. Then the woman said, Let thine handmaid, I pray thee, speak one word unto my lord the king. And he said, Say on.

And the woman said, Wherefore then hast thou thought such a thing against the people of God? for the king doth speak this thing as one which is faulty, in that the king doth not fetch home again his banished. For we must needs die, and are as water spilt on the ground, which cannot be gathered up again; neither doth God respect any person: yet doth he devise means, that his banished be not expelled from him. Now therefore that I am come to speak of this thing unto my lord the king, it is because the people have made me afraid: and thy handmaid said, I will now speak unto the king; it may be that the king will perform the request of his handmaid. For the king will hear, to deliver his handmaid out of the hand of the man that would destroy me and my son together out of the inheritance of God. Then thine handmaid said, The word of my lord the king shall now be comfortable: for as an angel of God, so is my lord the king to discern good and bad: therefore the LORD thy God will be with thee.

Then the king answered and said unto the woman, Hide not from me, I pray thee, the thing that I shall ask thee. And the woman said, Let my lord the king now speak. And the king said, Is not the hand of Joab with thee in all this? And the woman answered and said, As thy soul liveth, my lord the king, *none can turn to the right hand or to the left from ought that my lord the king hath spoken: for thy servant Joab, he bade me, and he put all these words in the mouth of thine handmaid: to fetch about this form of speech hath thy servant Joab done this thing: and my lord is wise, according to the wisdom of an angel of God, to know all things that are in the earth.*

And the king said unto Joab, Behold now, I have done this thing: go therefore, bring the young man Absalom again. And Joab fell to the ground on his face, and bowed himself, and thanked the king: and Joab said, To day thy servant knoweth that I have found grace in thy sight, my lord, O king, in that the king hath fulfilled the request of his servant. So Joab arose and went to Geshur, and brought Absalom to Jerusalem. And the king said, Let him turn to his own house, and let him not see my face. So Absalom returned to his own house, and saw not the king's face.

But in all Israel there was none to be so much praised as Absalom for his beauty: from the sole of his foot even to the crown of his head there was no blemish in him. And when he polled his head, (for it was at every year's end that he polled it: because the hair was heavy on him, therefore he polled it:) he weighed the hair of his head at two hundred shekels after the king's weight. And unto Absalom there were born three sons, and one daughter, whose name was Tamar: she was a woman of a fair countenance.

So Absalom dwelt two full years in Jerusalem, and saw not the king's face. Therefore Absalom sent for Joab, to have sent him to the king; but he would not come to him: and when he sent again the second time, he would not come. Therefore he said unto his servants, See, Joab's field is near mine, and he hath barley there; go and set it on fire. And Absalom's servants set the field on fire. Then Joab arose, and came to Absalom unto his house, and said unto him, Wherefore have thy servants set my field on fire?

And Absalom answered Joab, Behold, I sent unto thee, saying, Come hither, that I may send thee to the king, to say, Wherefore am I come from Geshur? it had been good for me to have been there still: now therefore let me see the king's face; and if there be any iniquity in me, let him kill me. So Joab came to the king, and told him: and when he had called for Absalom, he came to the king, and bowed himself on his face to the ground before the king: and the king kissed Absalom.

(2 Samuel 14)

❧✦❧

Bad things happen when we fail to follow God's directions. David loved his children very much, but to a fault. He did exactly what Solomon—ironically, David's own son—cautions against in Proverbs: he failed to correct them (Proverbs 13:14). Had David obeyed God and applied the Mosaic Law to his son Amnon for his sin against his sister, Absalom would not have found it necessary to avenge his sister's rape. In addition, had David dealt with Absalom according to Exodus 21:12, by putting him to death for the murder of his brother Amnon, and not brought him back to Jerusalem, the repercussions in 2 Samuel 18 could have been avoided. We ought to love others in spite of their flaws; after all, God loves us despite our shortcomings. But if you spare the rod, you will spoil the child, and shame, sorrow, and death will be the end result. Discipline, consequences, boundaries, a clear sense of right and wrong, with a heap of love, are necessary for raising our children.

Many times, we find what God asks us to do in regards to sin quite hard, jarring even. For example, the Bible says, *"If your hand or foot offends you [causes you to sin], cut it off"* (Matthew 18:8), and *"if your right eye offends you [causes you to sin], gouge it out"* (Matthew 5:29). While this is not meant literally, we certainly see the need to take drastic action when it comes to dealing with anything that causes us to sin, or that goes against God. Jesus explicitly states why such extreme measures, in the aforementioned warnings, are necessary: it is better to be without an arm or eye than it is to perish in hell. Sometimes, God requires us to deal thoroughly and decisively with things or people we view as being innocuous or harmless. He instructed the Children of Israel, when they were leaving Egypt, to drive out all the inhabitants of the land He was leading them to. He wanted them to thoroughly purge the land of its current residents and temples. He was trying to save His chosen from being influenced by, and falling into, the sinful practices of people whose god was not Yahweh (Exodus 23:20–33).

We don't always understand why God asks us to distance ourselves from certain people, or to completely destroy certain things, but the all-knowing God knows why He requires such actions, and when we fail to obey, the repercussions are deadly. Trust and obey His voice and leading.

Prayer: Father, I thank you for your divine leading. Please give me the strength to do whatever your Spirit leads me to do. I trust you. I know that you know all things and will only lead me in paths of righteousness. Strengthen me, dear Lord, In Jesus' name. Amen.

Selfless in Struggles

2 Samuel 15

And it came to pass after this, that Absalom prepared him chariots and horses, and fifty men to run before him. And Absalom rose up early, and stood beside the way of the gate: and it was so, that when any man that had a controversy came to the king for judgment, then Absalom called unto him, and said, Of what city art thou? And he said, Thy servant is of one of the tribes of Israel.

And Absalom said unto him, See, thy matters are good and right; but there is no man deputed of the king to hear thee. Absalom said moreover, Oh that I were made judge in the land, that every man which hath any suit or cause might come unto me, and I would do him justice!

And it was so, that when any man came nigh to him to do him obeisance, he put forth his hand, and took him, and kissed him. And on this manner did Absalom to all Israel that came to the king for judgment: so Absalom stole the hearts of the men of Israel.

And it came to pass after forty years, that Absalom said unto the king, I pray thee, let me go and pay my vow, which I have vowed unto the LORD, in Hebron. For thy servant vowed a vow while I abode at Geshur in Syria, saying, If the LORD shall bring me again indeed to Jerusalem, then I will serve the LORD.

And the king said unto him, Go in peace. So he arose, and went to Hebron. But Absalom sent spies throughout all the tribes of Israel, saying, As soon as ye hear the sound of the trumpet, then ye shall say, Absalom reigneth in Hebron.

And with Absalom went two hundred men out of Jerusalem, that were called; and they went in their simplicity, and they knew not any thing. And Absalom sent for Ahithophel the Gilonite, David's counsellor, from his city, even from Giloh, while he offered sacrifices. And the conspiracy was strong; for the people increased continually with Absalom.

And there came a messenger to David, saying, The hearts of the men of Israel are after Absalom. And David said unto all his servants that were with him at Jerusalem, Arise, and let us flee; for we shall not else escape from Absalom: make speed to depart, lest he overtake us suddenly, and bring evil upon us, and smite the city with the edge of the sword.

And the king's servants said unto the king, Behold, thy servants are ready to do whatsoever my lord the king shall appoint. And the king went forth, and all his household after him. And the king left ten women, which were concubines, to keep the house. And the king went forth, and all the people after him, and tarried in a place that was far off.

And all his servants passed on beside him; and all the Cherethites, and all the Pelethites, and all the Gittites, six hundred men which came after him from Gath, passed on before the king.

Then said the king to Ittai the Gittite, Wherefore goest thou also with us? return to thy place, and abide with the king: for thou art a stranger, and also an exile.

Whereas thou camest but yesterday, should I this day make thee go up and down with us? seeing I go whither I may, return thou, and take back thy brethren: mercy and truth be with thee. And Ittai answered the king, and said, As the LORD liveth, and as my lord the king liveth, surely in what place my lord the king shall be, whether in death or life, even there also will thy servant be. And David said to Ittai, Go and pass over. And Ittai the Gittite passed over, and all his men, and all the little ones that were with him. And all the country wept with a loud voice, and all the people passed over: the king also himself passed over the brook Kidron, and all the people passed over, toward the way of the wilderness.

(2 Samuel 15:1-23)

D espite the upheaval and turmoil David was facing, he was selfless. The king was a thoughtful and considerate leader, even when his situation was life-threatening. David would rather go into exile again, even with the possibility of never returning to his throne, in order to save Jerusalem from a bloodbath. David ran in order to save the people from the war that was bound to erupt when Absalom came to overthrow him. Had David desired, as a man of war with so many experienced and elite fighters, he could have stood his ground and won, but he judged the lives of the people as too high a price to pay. He put the people first; not his pride, his ego, or his feelings, but the people. David asked Ittai to return to the city, because he hadn't been with the king long enough to owe him that level of allegiance. He also maintained that the ark of the covenant needed to return to Jerusalem, even if that meant he would never see it again. In these instances, David's main preoccupation was the greater good of others.

David was selfless, thoughtful, and considerate, even in the midst of his own turmoil and betrayal. Going through rough situations is not a reason to mistreat others or to be selfish. Often, we use the fact that we are going through challenging times, or having a bad day, as justification to be less than kind to others or inconsiderate of others. We convince ourselves that due to our situation we have a right to be so preoccupied with our own problems that we become thoughtless of how our actions and words affect others. Putting others first, especially in difficult times, is not something that comes naturally to us. However, the Bible does admonish us not to be selfish but to be humble and value others above ourselves (Philippians 2:3). Love is always patient and kind, never self-seeking (1 Corinthians 13:4–8). Even Christ, in the midst of His agony, demonstrated love, forgiveness, and humility (Luke 23:34). Let us ask God daily to fill our hearts with that kind of love, so that despite our situations we may exhibit the love that pleases God.

Prayer: Father, in Jesus' name, I thank you for your unconditional love towards me. Please give me the grace to exhibit that same love to others. Help me to be kind, in words and deeds, even when my situations are less than ideal. Help me to be mindful of others and to esteem them higher than myself. Let the love of God and the fruit of the Spirit manifest in me always, in Jesus' name. Amen.

Decisions in Downtimes

2 Samuel 16:1–4 & 19:15–30

And when David was a little past the top of the hill, behold, Ziba the servant of Mephibosheth met him, with a couple of asses saddled, and upon them two hundred loaves of bread, and an hundred bunches of raisins, and an hundred of summer fruits, and a bottle of wine.

And the king said unto Ziba, What meanest thou by these? And Ziba said, The asses be for the king's household to ride on; and the bread and summer fruit for the young men to eat; and the wine, that such as be faint in the wilderness may drink.

And the king said, And where is thy master's son? And Ziba said unto the king, Behold, he abideth at Jerusalem: for he said, To day shall the house of Israel restore me the kingdom of my father.

Then said the king to Ziba, Behold, thine are all that pertained unto Mephibosheth. And Ziba said, I humbly beseech thee that I may find grace in thy sight, my lord, O king.

(2 Samuel 16:1–4)

So the king returned, and came to Jordan. And Judah came to Gilgal, to go to meet the king, to conduct the king over

Jordan. And Shimei the son of Gera, a Benjamite, which was of Bahurim, hasted and came down with the men of Judah to meet king David. And there were a thousand men of Benjamin with him, and Ziba the servant of the house of Saul, and his fifteen sons and his twenty servants with him; and they went over Jordan before the king.

And there went over a ferry boat to carry over the king's household, and to do what he thought good. And Shimei the son of Gera fell down before the king, as he was come over Jordan; and said unto the king, Let not my lord impute iniquity unto me, neither do thou remember that which thy servant did perversely the day that my lord the king went out of Jerusalem, that the king should take it to his heart. For thy servant doth know that I have sinned: therefore, behold, I am come the first this day of all the house of Joseph to go down to meet my lord the king.

But Abishai the son of Zeruiah answered and said, Shall not Shimei be put to death for this, because he cursed the LORD's anointed? And David said, What have I to do with you, ye sons of Zeruiah, that ye should this day be adversaries unto me? shall there any man be put to death this day in Israel? for do not I know that I am this day king over Israel?

Therefore the king said unto Shimei, Thou shalt not die. And the king sware unto him. And Mephibosheth the son of Saul came down to meet the king, and had neither dressed his feet, nor trimmed his beard, nor washed his clothes, from the day the king departed until the day he came again in peace. And it came to pass, when he was come to Jerusalem to meet the king, that the king said unto him, Wherefore wentest not thou with me, Mephibosheth? And he answered, My lord, O king, my servant deceived me: for thy servant said, I will saddle me an ass, that I may ride thereon, and go to the king; because thy servant is lame. And he hath slandered thy servant unto my lord the king; but my lord the king is as an angel of God: do therefore what is good in thine eyes. For all of my father's house were but dead men before my lord the king: yet didst thou set thy servant among them that did eat at thine own table. What right therefore have I yet to cry any more unto the king? And the king said unto him, Why speakest thou any more of thy matters? I have said, Thou and Ziba divide the land. And Mephibosheth said unto the king, Yea, let him take all, forasmuch as my lord the king is come again in peace unto his own house.

(2 Samuel 19:15–30)

And Mephibosheth the son of Saul came down to meet the king, and had neither dressed his feet, nor trimmed his beard, nor washed his clothes, from the day the king departed until the day he came again in peace. And it came to pass, when he was come to Jerusalem to meet the king, that the king said unto him, Wherefore wentest not thou with me, Mephibosheth?

And he answered, My lord, O king, my servant deceived me: for thy servant said, I will saddle me an ass, that I may ride thereon, and go to the king; because thy servant is lame.

And he hath slandered thy servant unto my lord the king; but my lord the king is as an angel of God: do therefore what is good in thine eyes. For all of my father's house were but dead men before my lord the king: yet didst thou set thy servant among them that did eat at thine own table. What right therefore have I yet to cry any more unto the king?

And the king said unto him, Why speakest thou any more of thy matters? I have said, Thou and Ziba divide the land.

And Mephibosheth said unto the king, Yea, let him take all, forasmuch as my lord the king is come again in peace unto his own house.

(2 Samuel 19:15–30)

n the midst of his latest trial, David must have been battling feelings of betrayal, hurt, and disappointment that his own son, Absalom, and former advisor, Ahithophel, both of whom he trusted, were rising up against him to destroy him. It is no wonder that he lacked discernment and fell prey to a conniving liar, Ziba, who only bore news of someone else's alleged betrayal to an already hurting David. Without mulling it over or seeking God, a bruised David made the wrong decision. Blinded by his turmoil and, possibly, feelings of insecurity, David failed to see Ziba's real aim, which was to take advantage of the situation for his own gain. Ziba's heartless motive was to use David's downtime and pain as an opportunity for self-advancement.

David faced another dilemma when it came time to discern the truth and judge between two conflicting stories from Mephibosheth (19:24–29) and Ziba (16:1–4). Ironically, David showed more grace to the one who had cursed him to his face—Ziba—than to the one who he was told betrayed him—Mephibosheth. Here David definitely judged incorrectly, but it's no wonder, because in these grey areas, David never sought the wisdom and guidance of God.

In our downtimes, we are most vulnerable and, therefore, ought to be extremely cautious about the decisions we make in those seasons. Hurt, strong emotions, and places of vulnerability can cause us to make unwise decisions, which we may come to regret when the dust settles and wisdom starts ruling again. In times when life-changing decisions are to be made about confusing circumstances, it is hard not to remember David's son Solomon (1 Kings 3:1–28). Solomon was only able take the right course of action because he sought God's wisdom. Sometimes you just don't know what God wants. When you are faced with a dilemma, or any decision where the will of God is unclear, it is imperative that you pause and seek God. You are to hold off, if you can, until you decipher what God wants you to do. The least you should do is pray about it, asking God for guidance.

When you really don't know what God wants, and an immediate decision is critical, pray! Ask God to lead the way, order your steps, open doors that He has ordained, and close forbidden doors. If there is no immediate answer that you can decipher, step out in faith and ask Him to work it out in the end for your good and for His glory.

Prayer: Lord, teach me how to pause and seek your face. Impart wisdom and discernment to me that I may see the truth at all times. Order my steps, oh God, so that I may walk in the spirit and so that all things will work together for my good and for your glory. Amen.

Grace for Grace

2 Samuel 16:5–13 & 19:19–23

And when king David came to Bahurim, behold, thence came out a man of the family of the house of Saul, whose name was Shimei, the son of Gera: he came forth, and cursed still as he came. And he cast stones at David, and at all the servants of king David: and all the people and all the mighty men were on his right hand and on his left.

And thus said Shimei when he cursed, Come out, come out, thou bloody man, and thou man of Belial: The LORD hath returned upon thee all the blood of the house of Saul, in whose stead thou hast reigned; and the LORD hath delivered the kingdom into the hand of Absalom thy son: and, behold, thou art taken in thy mischief, because thou art a bloody man.

Then said Abishai the son of Zeruiah unto the king, Why should this dead dog curse my lord the king? Let me go over, I pray thee, and take off his head.

And the king said, What have I to do with you, ye sons of Zeruiah? so let him curse, because the LORD hath said unto him, Curse David. Who shall then say, Wherefore hast thou done so?

And David said to Abishai, and to all his servants, Behold, my son, which came forth of my bowels, seeketh my life: how much more now may this Benjamite do it? Let him alone, and let him curse; for the Lord *hath bidden him. It may be that the* Lord *will look on mine affliction, and that the* Lord *will requite me good for his cursing this day.*

And as David and his men went by the way, Shimei went along on the hill's side over against him, and cursed as he went, and threw stones at him, and cast dust.

(2 Samuel 16:5–13)

And said unto the king, Let not my lord impute iniquity unto me, neither do thou remember that which thy servant did perversely the day that my lord the king went out of Jerusalem, that the king should take it to his heart.

For thy servant doth know that I have sinned: therefore, behold, I am come the first this day of all the house of Joseph to go down to meet my lord the king. But Abishai the son of Zeruiah answered and said, Shall not Shimei be put to death for this, because he cursed the Lord's *anointed?*

And David said, What have I to do with you, ye sons of Zeruiah, that ye should this day be adversaries unto me? shall there any man be put to death this day in Israel? For do not I know that I am this day king over Israel? Therefore the king said unto Shimei, Thou shalt not die. And the king sware unto him.

(2 Samuel 19:19–23)

Davavid was attacked by Shimei when he was at an extremely low point. On the run from his son who sought to kill him, David was so broken and humbled. There is no doubt the king remembered the judgement that God had pronounced upon his household because of his sin with Bathsheba (2 Samuel 12:10–12). At this point, David probably did not see himself as a powerful king who could easily destroy the life of the one cursing him, but as a wretched man whose own actions had made his current situation justifiable. The king in exile would not even avenge himself, even though He could. David's broken response to the outrageous actions of his enemy was essentially, "Whatever I'm going through, if it is of God, then it cannot be stopped, and if it is not of God, then He will restore me." When God did restore David, he clearly felt unworthy to impose judgement on another. Recognizing that God had been gracious to him, the king decided to be gracious to Shimei also. He was so broken and overwhelmed after all that God had done to restore him that David's best response to Shimei's plea for mercy was *grace for grace*. David felt that he should impute forgiveness and grace rather than judgement and condemnation, because that is what God had given him, although David, on his deathbed, instructed his son Solomon to deal with Shemei (1 Kings 2:8–9).

Many times, people are the visible source of our brokenness and turmoil, or they exacerbate our pain in one way or another. The natural tendency when we're out of the fire is not to forgive those who worked against our restoration. But grace for grace should be our response. The steps of a good person are ordered by God (Psalm 37:23). So if He allows us to go through harrowing situations and others are somehow contributing parts of that experience, when we are restored, we ought to forgive them. God's purpose in our trials will never be to leave us bitter or resentful. While we may have to re-examine relationships after trials, forgiveness is crucial. Grace for grace. If God restored you and brought you through, let that undeserved grace guide your actions when dealing with others.

Prayer: Father, I thank you for grace. I thank you that even when my trials are a result of my sinful actions, you still find a way to bring me out. Help me to extend that same grace to those whose actions, or lack thereof, have caused me pain. Give me a heart that forgives, and a love that covers a multitude of sins, in Jesus' name. Amen.

Favour Comes From God

2 Samuel 19:13

And say ye to Amasa, Art thou not of my bone, and of my flesh? God do so to me, and more also, if thou be not captain of the host before me continually in the room of Joab.

(2 Samuel 19:13)

───◈───

D avid's message to Amasa was unwise, to say the least. The man being promised the position of captain of the king's army was first the captain of the king's enemy's army (2 Samuel 17:25). It is doubtless that David thought Amasa had the power and influence he needed in order to win back Judah. David was willing to compromise good sense, forgetting that God had already ordained and anointed him as king (1 Samuel 16:12–13). By operating under the assumption that he had to cater to and appease an enemy in order to take up his rightful place, David was minimizing all that God had done for him in the past to keep him safe from his numerous enemies—from Goliath to Absalom—and to bring him to the throne. Favour, as David should have known, is given by God.

The temptation to cater to and appease those whom we assume have the power and influence to promote us can be powerful at times. But you cannot compromise to win favour. God is the one who promotes and gives power, and He is the one who demotes and takes power away. We should not be overly concerned about whether people like us or approve of us, because that leads to compromise. Our focus should be pleasing God and staying in His will, and He will give us favour, even with our enemies, and in unexpected places. Even when our enemies seem stronger than we are, we must not compromise to please. Remember the story of Balaam who was hired by the king to curse Israel? Every time he tried to pronounce a curse on God's people, a pronouncement of blessings came forth instead (Numbers 23–24). God will bless us and give us favour, despite those who are against us. Do not compromise divine wisdom to seek favour, like David did. As a child of God, there is no need. Scripture reminds us that we are to *"Trust in the Lord with all [our] hearts and lean not to [our] own understanding. In all [our] ways acknowledge Him and He shall direct [our] paths"* (Proverbs 3:5–6).

Prayer: Father in Heaven, I thank you for favour. Thank you, Lord, that you have already ordained blessings for my life and that no one can curse whom you have blessed. Help me to walk in the knowledge of your faithfulness and not to compromise by appeasing others in order to obtain favour from them. My help, blessings, and success come from you, and I thank you, in Jesus' name. Amen.

No Weapon Formed Shall Prosper!

2 Samuel 22

And David spake unto the Lord the words of this song in the day that the Lord had delivered him out of the hand of all his enemies, and out of the hand of Saul: and he said, The Lord is my rock, and my fortress, and my deliverer; the God of my rock; in him will I trust: he is my shield, and the horn of my salvation, my high tower, and my refuge, my saviour; thou savest me from violence. I will call on the Lord, who is worthy to be praised: so shall I be saved from mine enemies.

When the waves of death compassed me, the floods of ungodly men made me afraid; the sorrows of hell compassed me about; the snares of death prevented me; in my distress I called upon the Lord, and cried to my God: and he did hear my voice out of his temple, and my cry did enter into his ears. Then the earth shook and trembled; the foundations of heaven moved and shook, because he was wroth.

There went up a smoke out of his nostrils, and fire out of his mouth devoured: coals were kindled by it. He bowed the heavens also, and came down; and darkness was under his feet.

And he rode upon a cherub, and did fly: and he was

seen upon the wings of the wind. And he made darkness pavilions round about him, dark waters, and thick clouds of the skies. Through the brightness before him were coals of fire kindled. The LORD thundered from heaven, and the most High uttered his voice.

And he sent out arrows, and scattered them; lightning, and discomfited them. And the channels of the sea appeared, the foundations of the world were discovered, at the rebuking of the LORD, at the blast of the breath of his nostrils. He sent from above, he took me; he drew me out of many waters; He delivered me from my strong enemy, and from them that hated me: for they were too strong for me.

They prevented me in the day of my calamity: but the LORD was my stay. He brought me forth also into a large place: he delivered me, because he delighted in me. The LORD rewarded me according to my righteousness: according to the cleanness of my hands hath he recompensed me.

For I have kept the ways of the LORD, and have not wickedly departed from my God. For all his judgments were before me: and as for his statutes, I did not depart from them.

I was also upright before him, and have kept myself from mine iniquity. Therefore the LORD hath recompensed me according to my righteousness; according to my cleanness in his eye sight. With the merciful thou wilt shew thyself merciful, and with the upright man thou wilt shew thyself upright.

(2 Samuel 22:1–26)

2 Samuel 22 comes out of the depths of the soul of a man

who had been through many battles. Much of David's lifetime was marked with war, conflict, and opposition, yet, because of Jehovah, David died, not in war or battle, but from old age. David was a living testament of the truth of Isaiah's prophetic word that *"No weapon formed against you shall prosper"* (Isaiah 54:17).

As believers, we understand that the prophecy does not eliminate the formation of weapons, just their ability to prosper. Numerous weapons were formed and sharpened against David, and some seemed destined to prosper, but the Lord of Hosts brought every weapon to nought. Some battles will be notable for their formidable opponents from the enemy's camp, like Goliath (1 Samuel 17). There are some battles that will be prolonged and bitter, even because of the unwillingness to retaliate, like the situation with Saul (1 Samuel 18–28). Some battles will be marked by betrayal from within the camp, like Absalom (2 Samuel 15) and Sheba (2 Samuel 20). True to prophecy, every one of David's enemies was defeated. Not only were they defeated, but they also died violent deaths, sometimes to the distress of David. When David refused to fight back and avenge himself, God intervened and brought about his enemies' end.

In this life, many weapons will be formed against the children of God. Some we will willingly engage in, like David and Goliath, and some we will attempt to run away from, like David's conflicts with Saul and Absalom. One thing is certain: Jehovah Sabaoth will fight all our battles, and Jehovah Nissi will be a banner round about us to protect us from the enemy. At the end of it all, like David, we will be victorious. We are more than conquerors (Romans 8:37), and every force that opposes us, regardless of what realm they are in, will be defeated. Furthermore, we will condemn every tongue that rises up against us (Isaiah 54:17). Remind your enemy daily that the LORD your God will not allow anyone to oppress you. He will rebuke kings for [your] sake, saying, *"Touch not my anointed, and do my prophet no harm"* (1 Chronicles 16:21–22).

Prayer: Father, thank you for the assurance of victory. God, I believe, according to your Word, that no weapon formed against me shall prosper. Give me strength in times of struggle to remember that you are fighting for me, in Jesus' name. Amen.

Trials, Reflection, Worship

2 Samuel 22

With the pure thou wilt shew thyself pure; and with the froward thou wilt shew thyself unsavoury. And the afflicted people thou wilt save: but thine eyes are upon the haughty, that thou mayest bring them down. For thou art my lamp, O LORD: and the LORD will lighten my darkness. For by thee I have run through a troop: by my God have I leaped over a wall. As for God, his way is perfect; the word of the LORD is tried: he is a buckler to all them that trust in him. For who is God, save the LORD? and who is a rock, save our God? God is my strength and power: and he maketh my way perfect. He maketh my feet like hinds' feet: and setteth me upon my high places. He teacheth my hands to war; so that a bow of steel is broken by mine arms. Thou hast also given me the shield of thy salvation: and thy gentleness hath made me great.

Then did I beat them as small as the dust of the earth, I did stamp them as the mire of the street, and did spread them abroad. Thou also hast delivered me from the strivings of my people, thou hast kept me to be head of the heathen: a people which I knew not shall serve me. Strangers shall submit themselves unto me: as soon as they hear, they shall be obedient unto me. Strangers shall fade away, and they shall be afraid out of their close places. The LORD liveth; and blessed be my rock; and exalted be the God of the rock of my salvation. It is God that avengeth me, and that bringeth down the people under me. And that bringeth me forth from mine enemies: thou also hast lifted me up on high above them that rose up against me: thou hast delivered me from the violent man. Therefore I will give thanks unto thee, O Lord, among the heathen, and I will sing praises unto thy name. He is the tower of salvation for his king: and sheweth mercy to his anointed, unto David, and to his seed for evermore.

(2 Samuel 22:27–51)

———◆◆◆———

This chapter of 2 Samuel represents, what I consider to be, the most emulative characteristic of David. He was a worshipper, truly a man after God's own heart. David never failed to stand in awe of God and His glory. The Book of Psalms is filled with similar tributes to God. He gushed over the goodness of God, and stood securely in the love of God for him and the power of God to deliver him. His tribute to God was flowery and heartfelt, like one who has had a real encounter with the true and living God. He never forgot the goodness of God, and always made his boast in the Lord God of his salvation. Notably, David's celebration of God came with accurate reflection following devastating trials.

Trials are an inescapable fact of life. In fact, David states in Psalm 34:19, *"Many are the afflictions of the righteous."* And Jesus himself says in John 16:33, *"In the world you shall have tribulation."* However, when the Lord "delivers [you] out of them all," because Jesus Christ has "overcome the world" (John 16:33), it does the soul well to reflect on what you have been through and where God has brought you from. Reflection puts experiences and emotions into words. It examines lessons learned and often reveals new information about ourselves, those around us, and our God. It is almost impossible to learn every lesson, or see everything clearly while in the midst of a trial, but it is true that hindsight is 20/20. And no believer who has been through a trial, and reflects on the ways that God has made, the doors He has opened and shut, the favour He has doled out, and the delivering power He has manifested can fail to worship Him. The more we think about the goodness of God, the more gratitude wells up on the inside of us. The more we reflect on the ways of God, the clearer and more meaningful the names and attributes of God become. After trials and reflection, no longer do we just see Him as a deliverer, provider, way-maker because of vicarious experiences, but now we *know* that He is because He has done it for us. This knowing intensifies our worship, sweetens our praise, and fills our hearts with wonder at the awesomeness of our God.

When you are going through trials, do not despair. God is showing you aspects of Himself you will never fully comprehend until you've been there. Be sure to reflect on what God has done, and who He is, and the spirit of worship, the security of knowledge, and the heart of praise will forever be your portion.

Prayer: Father, I thank you for showing yourself strong in every trial. Help me to never miss the many ways you come through for me, and may my worship and praise come up to you as a sweet-smelling savour. Amen.

Ruling in the Fear of God

2 Samuel 23:3

The God of Israel said, the Rock of Israel spake to me, He that ruleth over men must be just, ruling in the fear of God.
(2 Samuel 23:3)

―――❖❖❖―――

As a man of great experience leading the people of God, David was certainly qualified to expound on the characteristics of a leader. As per David, *"He that ruleth over men must be just, ruling in the fear of God"* (2 Samuel 23:3). As in the case of most people who know that death is imminent, their last words are usually very well thought out and deemed important by both the speaker and hearer. Knowing that kingship was now to be passed to Solomon, his son, David's first charge to him was to rule and walk in the ways of God. Clearly, David knew that reliance on and obedience to God was the key to successful leadership, and that is what he wanted to leave Solomon with. These two kings were excellent testimonies of the benefit of ruling in the fear of God. David, who inquired of God most times and had a heart for the work and the people of God, was made to prosper, given victory over his enemies, and called "a man after [God's] own heart" (1 Samuel 13:14). When he stepped outside the fear of God and made decisions in accordance to the flesh, he felt the wrath of God (see 2 Samuel 24). Had Solomon taken heed to his father's instructions to rule in the fear of God, he would not have been so severely chastised by God (1 Kings 11).

A position of authority is no light matter or undertaking. In the secular world, leadership is serious business, and that seriousness is only heightened when it comes to leadership in the kingdom of God. Leadership of God's people is to be taken up humbly and reverently, with the leader depending completely on God for guidance and wisdom. Rulers must make God their source; they must be acutely aware that others are looking to them as examples of what it means to walk closely with God and to hear from Him. Ultimately, leaders must be able to say, "Follow me as I follow Christ." The aforementioned can only happen when those in authority rule in the fear of God. It is when we fail to walk in the fear of God that we end up sinning against God or behaving in unscrupulous ways that make others question or doubt our faith and our God. As a leader, the mere understanding that your action can have such devastating consequences in the kingdom of God should drive the fear of God into you and cause you to take your charge very seriously.

Prayer: Lord, I recognize that you are the one who appoints and takes down leaders. In every leadership role you entrust me with, may I recognize the importance of my charge and put you at the helm of it all. May those I lead see Christ in me and experience strengthened relationships with you, because I depend on you, in Jesus' name. Amen.

Mighty Man or Woman of Valour

2 Samuel 23:8–39

These be the names of the mighty men whom David had: The Tachmonite that sat in the seat, chief among the captains; the same was Adino the Eznite: he lift up his spear against eight hundred, whom he slew at one time. And after him was Eleazar the son of Dodo the Ahohite, one of the three mighty men with David, when they defied the Philistines that were there gathered together to battle, and the men of Israel were gone away: he arose, and smote the Philistines until his hand was weary, and his hand clave unto the sword: and the LORD wrought a great victory that day; and the people returned after him only to spoil. And after him was Shammah the son of Agee the Hararite. And the Philistines were gathered together into a troop, where was a piece of ground full of lentiles: and the people fled from the Philistines. But he stood in the midst of the ground, and defended it, and slew the Philistines: and the LORD wrought a great victory.

And three of the thirty chief went down, and came to David in the harvest time unto the cave of Adullam: and the troop of the Philistines pitched in the valley of Rephaim. And

David was then in an hold, and the garrison of the Philistines was then in Bethlehem. And David longed, and said, Oh that one would give me drink of the water of the well of Bethlehem, which is by the gate! And the three mighty men brake through the host of the Philistines, and drew water out of the well of Bethlehem, that was by the gate, and took it, and brought it to David: nevertheless he would not drink thereof, but poured it out unto the LORD.

And he said, Be it far from me, O LORD, that I should do this: is not this the blood of the men that went in jeopardy of their lives? therefore he would not drink it. These things did these three mighty men. And Abishai, the brother of Joab, the son of Zeruiah, was chief among three. And he lifted up his spear against three hundred, and slew them, and had the name among three. Was he not most honourable of three? therefore he was their captain: howbeit he attained not unto the first three.

And Benaiah the son of Jehoiada, the son of a valiant man, of Kabzeel, who had done many acts, he slew two lionlike men of Moab: he went down also and slew a lion in the midst of a pit in time of snow: and he slew an Egyptian, a goodly man: and the Egyptian had a spear in his hand; but he went down to him with a staff, and plucked the spear out of the Egyptian's hand, and slew him with his own spear. These things did Benaiah the son of Jehoiada, and had the name among three mighty men. He was more honourable than the thirty, but he attained not to the first three. And David set him over his guard.

Asahel the brother of Joab was one of the thirty; Elhanan the son of Dodo of Bethlehem, Shammah the Harodite, Elika the Harodite, Helez the Paltite, Ira the son of Ikkesh the Tekoite, Abiezer the Anethothite, Mebunnai the Hushathite, Zalmon the Ahohite, Maharai the Netophathite, Heleb the son of Baanah, a Netophathite, Ittai the son of Ribai out of Gibeah of the children of Benjamin, Benaiah the Pirathonite, Hiddai of the brooks of Gaash, Abialbon the Arbathite, Azmaveth the Barhumite, Eliahba the Shaalbonite, of the sons of Jashen, Jonathan, Shammah the Hararite, Ahiam the son of Sharar the Hararite, Eliphelet the son of Ahasbai, the son of the Maachathite, Eliam the son of Ahithophel the Gilonite, Hezrai the Carmelite, Paarai the Arbite, Igal the son of Nathan of Zobah, Bani the Gadite, Zelek the Ammonite, Nahari the Beerothite, armourbearer to Joab the son of Zeruiah, Ira an Ithrite, Gareb an Ithrite, Uriah the Hittite: thirty and seven in all.

(2 Samuel 23:8–39)

What an honour it is to be listed among the mighty. David had many followers and many men who served him during his time, but here some of the exceptional ones are listed. They are remembered and established forever in the Bible as "mighty men." It is highly unlikely that any of these men imagined the reach of their valiant acts. They never conceived that they would be highly regarded and that their names would be written down in the Word of God and be read countless times, over thousands of years, by numerous eyes. They just lived to serve the king and did whatever was required of them, even if it cost them their lives.

What will your name be called for in the kingdom of God? What mighty deeds will you do for God? Will you slay spiritual giants, be an armour bearer, deliver many from the hands of the enemy? What will your legacy be? Unlike David, I am sure that God's scope, as it pertains to being mighty, is much broader. It is not limited to fighting in physical wars or with physical weapons.

Whatever you do for the kingdom of God will be recorded by God, and is precious in His sight. The moral of the story? Do something! We all have a God-given purpose for being here on Earth, fulfill that. Don't be idle. Don't consider other people's mighty acts as more valuable or worthwhile than anything you could do and, therefore, do nothing. Don't look at what giants others are slaying and despise, or count as less worthy, your immobilization of dwarfs. The only purpose you can fulfill is your own. The only purpose God has given you grace—divine enablement—to fulfil is your own. Be the mighty man or woman that God has called you to be. Let the ministry that God has birthed in you reach the souls that God has ordained for it to reach, and your name will be remembered, or called, as one who lived in the service of God. And even if no one else remembers your name, rest assured that God will. For as the Scripture says, *"God is not unrighteous to forget your work and labour of love, which ye have shewed toward his name, in that ye have ministered to the saints, and do minister"* (Hebrews 6:10).

Prayer: Father in Heaven, I want to be mighty in the works of God. Use me in your kingdom to fulfill your purpose and be a blessing to others. I want to be remembered as one who was used by God and excelled in the calling of God for my life. Give me grace to keep my eyes on you and my ears open to your voice, in Jesus' name. Amen.

The Sin of Pride

2 Samuel 24:1–9

And again the anger of the LORD was kindled against Israel, and he moved David against them to say, Go, number Israel and Judah.

For the king said to Joab the captain of the host, which was with him, Go now through all the tribes of Israel, from Dan even to Beersheba, and number ye the people, that I may know the number of the people.

And Joab said unto the king, Now the LORD thy God add unto the people, how many soever they be, an hundredfold, and that the eyes of my lord the king may see it: but why doth my lord the king delight in this thing?

Notwithstanding the king's word prevailed against Joab, and against the captains of the host. And Joab and the captains of the host went out from the presence of the king, to number the people of Israel.

And they passed over Jordan, and pitched in Aroer, on the right side of the city that lieth in the midst of the river of Gad, and toward Jazer: then they came to Gilead, and to the land of Tahtimhodshi; and they came to Danjaan, and about to Zidon, and came to the strong hold of Tyre, and to all the cities of the Hivites, and of the Canaanites: and they went out to the south *of Judah, even to Beersheba.*

So when they had gone through all the land, they came to Jerusalem at the end of nine months and twenty days. And Joab gave up the sum of the number of the people unto the king: and there were in Israel eight hundred thousand valiant men that drew the sword; and the men of Judah were five hundred thousand men.

(2 Samuel 24:1–9)

The chosen king, David, divinely appointed ruler of the people of the Most High God, decided to take a census. In today's age, with a census being such a commonplace practice, this decision seems innocuous enough. Even in those days, taking a census was not forbidden. In Numbers 1:2–3 and 26:2, God Himself had requested that Moses take a census of those able to go to war. What was flawed about David's decision to do this census was his motive—*"That I may know"* (v. 24). In a time when the strength of one's army, and the number of mighty, able-bodied men available for war was a great asset to a kingdom, David sought a cause for which to boast and feel contentment that no army could defeat his. We know David as an amazing warrior who led his army into many victories, and at this point, it almost seems as though he just wanted to sit back and gaze with pride at what he had and what he had accomplished. The sin of pride.

Beware of the things you do simply to boost your pride, make yourself feel important, and feed your ego. We must beware of situations that simply inflate our ego and cause us to think more highly of ourselves than we should. Attempts at flattery, and even genuine compliments, must always be met with the humbling thought that we are nothing without God, nor can we do anything without Him. It does not matter whether we have a whole lot or precious little, we must always remember that it's not by might nor by power but by the Spirit of God (Zechariah 4:6), which makes what we have, or who we are, and what we have accomplished inconsequential.

God hates pride, and the Word of God in regards to pride is enough to invoke the fear of God in any person— *"Pride goes before destruction and a haughty spirit before a fall"* (Proverbs 16:18); *"God opposes the proud but gives grace to the humble"* (James 4:6); *"The Lord has a day in store for all the proud and lofty, he shall be brought low"* (Isaiah 2:12); *"The Lord tears down the house of the proud"* (Proverbs 15:25); *"Everyone that is proud in heart is an abomination unto the Lord"* (Proverbs 16:5).

Who can afford to be opposed by Almighty God? We cannot afford pride, so we must be vigilant and stand fast against anything that causes it to rise up in our lives.

Prayer: Lord, have mercy on me and remove every trace of pride from my life. I acknowledge that I am nothing without you, and everything that I am and have is a testament to your grace and excellence. Help me to walk humbly before you, so I may not be opposed by you. Amen.

A Repentant Heart and a Merciful God

2 Samuel 24:10–16

And David's heart smote him after that he had numbered the people. And David said unto the LORD, I have sinned greatly in that I have done: and now, I beseech thee, O LORD, take away the iniquity of thy servant; for I have done very foolishly.

For when David was up in the morning, the word of the LORD came unto the prophet Gad, David's seer, saying, Go and say unto David, Thus saith the LORD, I offer thee three things; choose thee one of them, that I may do it unto thee.

So Gad came to David, and told him, and said unto him, Shall seven years of famine come unto thee in thy land? or wilt thou flee three months before thine enemies, while they pursue thee? or that there be three days' pestilence in thy land? now advise, and see what answer I shall return to him that sent me.

And David said unto Gad, I am in a great strait: let us fall now into the hand of the LORD; for his mercies are great: and let me not fall into the hand of man.

So the LORD sent a pestilence upon Israel from the morning even to the time appointed: and there died of the people from

Dan even to Beersheba seventy thousand men. And when the angel stretched out his hand upon Jerusalem to destroy it, the LORD repented him of the evil, and said to the angel that destroyed the people, It is enough: stay now thine hand. And the angel of the LORD was by the threshingplace of Araunah the Jebusite.

(2 Samuel 24:10–16)

———⊰⊱———

Caught again in folly, David exhibited a quickness to repent, even before the prophet approached him. David seemed to be more sensitive to the Spirit than he was at the time of his sin with Bathsheba (2 Samuel 11–12). We must be quick to repent, no matter how foolish or unworthy our sin makes us feel. No matter how low we think we have gone, we must not allow the spirit of condemnation to keep us back from repentance. God's grace and mercy are from everlasting to everlasting (Psalm 103:17). He quickly forgave David, and even offered David the option to choose his punishment, imagine that.

David prayed to fall into the hands of God and not of man. It is ironic that the only One who is always holy and despises sin is also the One who is merciful and quick to forgive. Mortals, who constantly fall short of the glory of God, take longer to be merciful to others, are faster to condemn, and dole out harsher punishments for sins that none of us are immune to. Many of us have the tendency to act self-righteously and judge harshly, when we are the ones who should be compassionate and love others back to right standing with God. If the only requirement for God's forgiveness is a repentant heart, then who are we to withhold forgiveness from others? Since when are we above sin? If God can forgive, why can't we?

Even in punishment, God is merciful. He commanded the angel to stop, because it was not His will that any should perish but that all should come to repentance (2 Peter 3:9; Ezekiel 18:32). God despises sin, but He is also a God of love. He would rather extend grace and bring us back into right standing than destroy us in our sin. He gives us the option to stay and wallow in sin or to repent and live.

If we sin, we ought not wallow in it; we have an intercessor and mediator, Jesus Christ, who will advocate on our behalf before the Father (1 John 2:1; 1 Timothy 2:5–6). Be quick to repent, and the God of mercy will cast your sin in the depths of the sea (Micah 7:19).

Prayer: Father, in the name of Jesus, I thank you for grace. I recognize my shortcomings, and I repent of my iniquities. Forgive me, oh God, for every sin, both of omission and commission. Give me the grace to live holy. But if I fall short, help me to be sensitive to the Spirit, and to turn and live, in Jesus' name. Amen.

Inquiring of the Lord

1 Samuel 23:1–5; 1 Samuel 30;
2 Samuel 2:1; 5:19, 23

Then they told David, saying, Behold, the Philistines fight against Keilah, and they rob the threshing floors. Therefore David enquired of the LORD, saying, Shall I go and smite these Philistines? And the LORD said unto David, Go, and smite the Philistines, and save Keilah.

And David's men said unto him, Behold, we be afraid here in Judah: how much more then if we come to Keilah against the armies of the Philistines?

Then David enquired of the LORD yet again. And the LORD answered him and said, Arise, go down to Keilah; for I will deliver the Philistines into thine hand. So David and his men went to Keilah, and fought with the Philistines, and brought away their cattle, and smote them with a great slaughter. So David saved the inhabitants of Keilah.

(1 Samuel 23:1–5)

And it came to pass after this, that David enquired of the LORD, saying, Shall I go up into any of the cities of Judah? And the LORD said unto him, Go up. And David said, Whither shall I go up? And he said, Unto Hebron.

(2 Samuel 2:1)

And David enquired of the LORD, saying, Shall I go up to the Philistines? wilt thou deliver them into mine hand? And the LORD said unto David, Go up: for I will doubtless deliver the Philistines into thine hand. And when David enquired of the LORD, he said, Thou shalt not go up; but fetch a compass behind them, and come upon them over against the mulberry trees.

(2 Samuel 5:19, 23)

———◆◆◆———

This is one of the most profound lessons from David's life. Numerous times in the life of David, as recounted in the Books of Samuel, David inquired of the Lord. David displayed something that every believer should emulate—complete reliance on God.

Even though David was asked for help to save the underdogs from the Philistines, he sought the Lord first to see what His will was, knowing that the victory would only come if God was fighting with him (1 Samuel 23:1–5). The attack against the Philistines might have been a noble undertaking, possibly even considered by some as "the right thing to do;" but David did not take it to mean that God wanted him to engage in war at that time. Sometimes the solution to the problem facing us seems obvious, but beware of taking things at face value. David was a mighty man of valour who had fought and won many battles. Judging by the fear of David's men, the current situation was one in which the enemy had the military advantage. But David did not rely on his warrior prowess or on his own might. He relied on God. Regardless of what the situation looked like, God's directions would lead David's army right. David was firm in his faith that if God instructed them to go up against the enemy, then God would deliver the enemy into their hands. He did not allow fear to keep him from seeking God.

David had already been ordained as king, and he knew the hand of God was on his life, yet when the opportunity to take his place as king presented itself, after many tumultuous years, David inquired of the Lord (2 Samuel 2:1). He did not assume that it was time to take his place, although he had been anointed for it. He did not assume that this was the time when he would be rewarded for all his troubles by taking his place as king. He made no assumptions; he humbly sought God's direction.

In 1 Samuel 30, David was in the midst of an overwhelming crisis. Not only was he personally affected, but all his men were also affected and were angry at him. For many people, the answer to the situation David was going through would be obvious. He, of course, was a great man of war. He had fought and won many battles before the enemy took his wives and the people spoke of stoning him. Of course, to pursue the enemy would be the obvious answer, even if it was as a sign of bravado and to show guts as a leader.

Crisis can be defined as a sudden and tragic upheaval in someone's life, and he or she often requires a quick and decisive response. Often, the way we respond in a crisis has a lasting impact. So what did David do? He sought the Lord. He did not let his emotions force him into action. He did not let the pressure from his followers force him into action. He did not let his pride in thinking that he could fight and win this battle force him into action. In the midst of the crisis, David sought the will of God. He wanted to know what God wanted Him to do. Such utter dependence on the will of God is amazing. David didn't think, "Well, time is of the essence. I need to make a decision quickly before they get too far." He was willing to not go for his wives, and risk being stoned, if God had said, "Do not pursue them."

How do we respond in times of urgency and crisis? Do we feel pressured to react quickly? Do we go for the most obvious response? Or do we ask God, in the midst of the turmoil, "What is *your* will?" or "What should I do?" and wait on Him for the answer and way forward? Inquiring of God is essential for anyone who desires to be led by the Spirit of God. Inquiring of the Lord is crucial for anyone who only wants to do "it" once, and get it right. He is the all-wise God, and His ways are perfect. His path and instructions are beyond reproach, so inquire of Him.

In science, face validity is only one measurement of validity, and it is certainly not the most sophisticated or reliable. The situation may seem simple and appear as though you can deal with it in your own strength, using your own strategies, but inquire of God. The enemy is quick to pounce on the pride and haughtiness of believers, when we assume that a situation is simple enough to handle on our own, without God's help. The truth is, regardless of the circumstances, we need God. Remember, our victory will not come by our power or might, but by His Spirit. Inquire of God, even when you are afraid of what the answer might be. The men were incensed, and threatened to stone David, but David inquired of the Lord, knowing that His answer could be "No, do not pursue the men." Despite the prospective backlash of an unwanted answer, David inquired of the Lord.

But what do you do when you inquire of God and do not get a response? What do you do when all you hear is silence? What do you do when all you hear is the sound of your cry or your lament echoing from the ceiling? What do you do when you ask, and His response is not what you expected or wanted? What do you do? You trust God and what He has already said. The Word of God already said that the race is not for the swift neither is the battle for the strong but for those who will endure. This may be your endurance test in this season. The Word of God already said that you are to take up your cross. This may be your cross in this season. It may not be the answer you want, but you must trust that God is still sovereign. He is still almighty. He still has your best interest at heart (Psalm 84:11). All things will work together for good for those who are called according to His purpose (Romans 8:28). And even though you go through the fire, floods, and waters, they will not overwhelm you (Zechariah 3:19; Isaiah 43:2).

The truth is that the Word of God doesn't always bring instantaneous glee, but if you trust God you will have peace. Trust His already spoken Word that His grace is sufficient for you and that His strength is made perfect in your times of weakness (2 Corinthians 12:9). Even in the midst of turmoil, and apparently unanswered inquiries, if you trust what God has already said, then be anxious for nothing. Instead, let the peace of God that passes all understanding keep your heart and mind. (Philippians 4:6–7).

Prayer: Lord, teach me to inquire of you, regardless of what the situation may look like. It may seem commonsensical, or it may seem daunting, I may even fear the answer I will get, but help me to turn to you anyways. Give me grace so when I hear nothing or when I hear an answer that's not what I wanted to hear, I will trust that you are in control and that you have my best interest at heart. Teach me how to wait for answers, not to be rushed or anxious, but to wait in peace. Amen.

The Heart of a Man after God's Own Heart

2 Samuel 24:17–25

And David spake unto the LORD when he saw the angel that smote the people, and said, Lo, I have sinned, and I have done wickedly: but these sheep, what have they done? let thine hand, I pray thee, be against me, and against my father's house. And Gad came that day to David, and said unto him, Go up, rear an altar unto the LORD in the threshing floor of Araunah the Jebusite.

And David, according to the saying of Gad, went up as the LORD commanded. And Araunah looked, and saw the king and his servants coming on toward him: and Araunah went out, and bowed himself before the king on his face upon the ground.

And Araunah said, Wherefore is my lord the king come to his servant? And David said, To buy the threshing floor of thee, to build an altar unto the LORD, that the plague may be stayed from the people.

And Araunah said unto David, Let my lord the king take and offer up what seemeth good unto him: behold, here be oxen for burnt sacrifice, and threshing instruments and other instruments of the oxen for wood. All these things did Araunah, as a king, give unto the king.

And Araunah said unto the king, The LORD thy God accept thee. And the king said unto Araunah, Nay; but I will surely buy it of thee at a price: neither will I offer burnt offerings unto the LORD my God of that which doth cost me nothing. So David bought the threshing floor and the oxen for fifty shekels of silver.

And David built there an altar unto the LORD, and offered burnt offerings and peace offerings. So the LORD was intreated for the land, and the plague was stayed from Israel.

(2 Samuel 24:17–25)

W hat gets one the commendation of "a man after God's own heart" from God himself? The last verses of this last chapter of 2 Samuel exposes some qualities of David that certainly gained him that place of honour. David was humble. Humble enough to acknowledge his shortcomings, and bold enough to be willing to pay the price for his failures. He didn't seek to negate his responsibilities, or think it appropriate that others should pay for his sin. We know how much God values humility and despises pride (James 4:6).

David was an intercessor to the end. He was a leader who did not think too highly of himself and his post to cry out to God on behalf of those he ruled over. David had a heart for the people of God. Time and time again, he showed himself to be one who was willing to sacrifice his life, and his family's life, for God's people. Even early on in our introduction to David, this little shepherd boy was filled with righteous indignation that the people of God were being mocked by Goliath (1 Samuel 17). In order to avenge the people of God, and the name of God, he put his life on the line by facing a giant that even the seasoned men of war were afraid of. His attitude was reminiscent of Moses' leading rebellious people through the wilderness (Exodus 32:30–32).

David knew what a worthy offering to God consisted of. A holy and acceptable offering was one of sacrifice (v. 24). David wasn't interested in cutting corners when it came to pleasing God. He wasn't looking for an easy way out or the most efficient way. His desire to please God overrode all motivations of self or asset preservation. Regardless of the cost, an acceptable offering to God—a sacrificial offering—was his intent.

The most precious offering we can give to God is us—our affection, our lives, our hearts. Paul implores us to offer our bodies as living sacrifices, holy and acceptable unto God, which is our reasonable service (Romans 12:1). Humility pleases God. A broken and contrite heart God will not despise (Psalm 51:17).

Prayer: Lord, there is no greater honour than to be someone whom you regard. Your commendations are the only meaningful ones. Give me grace to please you, regardless of the cost. Let my life be lived in honour of you, so that in the end I may hear "Well done, thou good and faithful servant" (Matthew 25:23).

NOTES

NOTES

NOTES

<u>NOTES</u>

Connect with Adanna!

Facebook: Souled-Out Sista
Twitter: Souled-Out sista @Adanna_SOS
Instagram: Adanna_SOS. Adanna Phillip
YouTube: Souled-Out Sista Adanna Phillip

www.ingramcontent.com/pod-product-compliance
Lightning Source LLC
Chambersburg PA
CBHW072346090426
42741CB00012B/2944